EFFECTIVE ONLINE SEARCHING

BOOKS IN LIBRARY AND INFORMATION SCIENCE

A Series of Monographs and Textbooks

EDITOR

ALLEN KENT

School of Library and Information Science
University of Pittsburgh
Pittsburgh, Pennsylvania

Vol. 1 Classified Library of Congress Subject Headings, Volume 1—Classified List, *edited by James G. Williams, Martha L. Manheimer, and Jay E. Daily* (out of print; see Vol. 39, Part A)

Vol. 2 Classified Library of Congress Subject Headings, Volume 2—Alphabetic List, *edited by James G. Williams, Martha L. Manheimer, and Jay E. Daily* (out of print; see Vol. 39, Part B)

Vol. 3 Organizing Nonprint Materials, *by Jay E. Daily*

Vol. 4 Computer-Based Chemical Information, *edited by Edward McC. Arnett and Allen Kent*

Vol. 5 Style Manual: A Guide for the Preparation of Reports and Dissertations, *by Martha L. Manheimer*

Vol. 6 The Anatomy of Censorship, *by Jay E. Daily*

Vol. 7 Information Science: Search for Identity, *edited by Anthony Debons (out of print)*

Vol. 8 Resource Sharing in Libraries: Why • How • When • Next Action Steps, *edited by Allen Kent (out of print)*

Vol. 9 Reading the Russian Language: A Guide for Librarians and Other Professionals, *by Rosalind Kent*

Vol. 10 Statewide Computing Systems: Coordinating Academic Computer Planning, *edited by Charles Mosmann (out of print)*

Vol. 11 Using the Chemical Literature: A Practical Guide, *by Henry M. Woodburn*

Vol. 12 Cataloging and Classification: A Workbook, *by Martha L. Manheimer (out of print; see Vol. 30)*

Vol. 13 Multi-media Indexes, Lists, and Review Sources: A Bibliographic Guide, *by Thomas L. Hart, Mary Alice Hunt, and Blanche Woolls*

Vol. 14 Document Retrieval Systems: Factors Affecting Search Time, *by K. Leon Montgomery*

Vol. 15 Library Automation Systems, *by Stephen R. Salmon*

Vol. 16 Black Literature Resources: Analysis and Organization, *by Doris H. Clack*

Vol. 17 Copyright—Information Technology—Public Policy: Part I—Copyright—Public Policies; Part II—Public Policies—Information Technology, *by Nicholas Henry (out of print)*

Vol. 18 Crisis in Copyright, *by William Z. Nasri*

Vol. 19 Mental Health Information Systems: Design and Implementation, *by David J. Kupfer, Michael S. Levine, and John A. Nelson*

Vol. 20 Handbook of Library Regulations, *by Marcy Murphy and Claude J. Johns, Jr. (out of print)*

Vol. 21 Library Resource Sharing, *by Allen Kent and Thomas J. Galvin*

Vol. 22 Computers in Newspaper Publishing: User-Oriented Systems, *by Dineh Moghdam*

Vol. 23 The On-Line Revolution in Libraries, *edited by Allen Kent and Thomas J. Galvin*

Vol. 24 The Library as a Learning Service Center, *by Patrick R. Penland and Aleyamma Mathai*

Vol. 25 Using the Mathematical Literature: A Practical Guide, *by Barbara Kirsch Schaefer*

Vol. 26 Use of Library Materials: The University of Pittsburgh Study, *by Allen Kent et al.*

Vol. 27 The Structure and Governance of Library Networks, *edited by Allen Kent and Thomas J. Galvin*

Vol. 28 The Development of Library Collections of Sound Recordings, *by Frank W. Hoffmann*

Vol. 29 Furnishing the Library Interior, *by William S. Pierce*

Vol. 30 Cataloging and Classification: A Workbook Second Edition, Revised and Expanded, *by Martha L. Manheimer*

Vol. 31 Handbook of Computer-Aided Composition, *by Arthur H. Phillips*

Vol. 32 OCLC: Its Governance, Function, Financing, and Technology, *by Albert F. Maruskin*

Vol. 33 Scientific and Technical Information Resources, *by Krishna Subramanyam*

Vol. 34 An Author Index to Library of Congress Classification, Class P, Subclasses PN, PR, PS, PZ, General Literature, English and American Literature, Fiction in English, and Juvenile Belles Lettres, *by Alan M. Greenberg*

Vol. 35 Using the Biological Literature: A Practical Guide, *by Elisabeth B. Davis*

Vol. 36 An Introduction to Automated Literature Searching, *by Elizabeth P. Hartner*

Vol. 37 The Retrieval of Information in the Humanities and the Social Sciences: Problems as Aids to Learning, *edited by Thomas P. Slavens*

Vol. 38 The Information Professional: Survey of an Emerging Field, *by Anthony Debons, Donald W. King, Una Mansfield, and Donald L. Shirey*

Vol. 39 Classified Library of Congress Subject Headings, Second Edition: Part A–Classified List; Part B–Alphabetic List, *edited by James G. Williams, Martha L. Manheimer, and Jay E. Daily*

Vol. 40 Information Technology: Critical Choices for Library Decision-Makers, *edited by Allen Kent and Thomas J. Galvin*

Vol. 41 Structure and Subject Interaction: Toward a Sociology of Knowledge in the Social Sciences, *by Stephen Bulick*

Vol. 42 World Librarianship: A Comparative Study, *by Richard Krzys and Gaston Litton*

Vol. 43 Guide to the Successful Thesis and Dissertation: Conception to Publication: A Handbook for Students and Faculty, *by James E. Mauch and Jack W. Birch*

Vol. 44 Physical Disability: An Annotated Literature Guide, *edited by Phyllis C. Self*

Vol. 45 Effective Online Searching: A Basic Text, *by Christine L. Borgman, Dineh Moghdam, and Patti K. Corbett*

Additional Volumes in Preparation

EFFECTIVE ONLINE SEARCHING

A Basic Text

Christine L. Borgman
Graduate School of Library and Information Science
University of California, Los Angeles
Los Angeles, California

Dineh Moghdam
Computer Information Systems
Bentley College
Waltham, Massachusetts

Patti K. Corbett
Graduate School of Public Health Library
University of Pittsburgh
Pittsburgh, Pennsylvania

CRC Press
Taylor & Francis Group
Boca Raton London New York

CRC Press is an imprint of the
Taylor & Francis Group, an **informa** business

First published 1984 by Marcel Dekker, Inc

Published 2019 by CRC Press
Taylor & Francis Group
6000 Broken Sound Parkway NW, Suite 300
Boca Raton, FL 33487-2742

First issued in paperback 2019

ISBN-13: 978-0-367-45181-3 (pbk)
ISBN-13: 978-0-8247-7142-3 (hbk)

Visit the Taylor & Francis Web site at
http://www.taylorandfrancis.com

and the CRC Press Web site at
http://www.crcpress.com

Library of Congress Cataloging in Publication Data

Borgman, Christine L.,
Effective online searching

(Books in library and information science ; vol. 45)
Includes bibliographies and index.
1. On-line bibliographic searching. 2. Information retrieval. I. Moghdam, Dineh, . II. Corbett, Patti K. III. Title. IV. Series: Books in library and information science ; v. 45.
Z699.B629 1984 025.5'24 84-9409

ISBN: 978-0-8247-7142-3

In appreciation for their patience, perseverance, and moral support, this book is dedicated to our husbands

George M. Mood

Phillip J. Davis

Joel Bregman

Foreword

Vannevar Bush, in his widely read and frequently cited article, "As We May Think," identified in 1945* a fundamental problem, the solution of which eluded those who served information seekers by acquiring, organizing, retrieving, and disseminating the records of our society. Selection, or retrieval from human memory, is not oriented to alphabetical or numerical sequences; yet many conventional catalogs and indexes are arrayed in that way. Vannevar Bush was not optimistic that one could even hope that the associations which permit man to conceptualize could be duplicated artificially.

But it is thirty-nine years since the Bush article appeared in print. During that time the computer has emerged as a powerful tool for processing information. Associations can now indeed be made artificially; the results of such associations can be displayed faster than they can be read. And so, as commercial ser-

---

**Atlantic Monthly*, Vol. 176, July 1945, pp. 101-108.

vices have provided this capability more and more conveniently, an online revolution has taken place.

Many are attracted to online systems by the lure of technology— the symbiosis of people and machines, involving a computer terminal, a distant computer, and a communication system that brings the power of the computer to one's fingertips— typically, to a typewriter keyboard in one's customary work environment. Some are attracted by the ability to produce a bibliography on any topic, on demand, simply by "pushing a button."

Many perceive online information systems merely in terms of substitution of functions currently performed manually. But few systems can be installed beneficially without rethinking current functions so as to optimize service *objectives*. Those who engage in this process find the effective attainment of objectives inhibited by the heavy hand of tradition. Most difficult of all is achievement of the qualitative advantage of information delivery capability--which is the rationale for an online information system.

This advantage is achieved by the ability of a computer to "correlate" aspects of a search. There is a problem in attempting to make this ability clear. It is exceptionally difficult to describe a process or an "experience," especially since it appears deceptively simple to those who have not had the experience.

Man has been so conditioned by arrays and displays in alphabetic and numeric sequence that the promise of online systems is not realized. The challenge is how to recondition those who would use these systems so that they are indeed effective supplements to their own memory. It is this challenge that this book takes up.

Those who teach the use of online systems have been hampered by the lack of adequate textbook materials. The authors have addressed this lack in their work.

A final note, a personal one: it gives me extraordinary pleasure to work with former students, as they progress in promising careers following graduation. Two of the authors (Borgman and Moghdam) were infected with the online "bug" when they were graduate students at the University of Pittsburgh a number of years ago. I think they will agree that there is no effective antidote for this "bug."

Allen Kent
University of Pittsburgh

Preface

In the past ten years, librarians, information specialists, and researchers have made increasing use of online information retrieval systems, yet few comprehensive training materials have been available. A text is needed which treats information retrieval systems in a practical, tutorial manner. This book attempts to fill that need, as a basic text concerned with the concepts and skills necessary to search online systems effectively.

The book is intended primarily for those who will act as search intermediaries, accepting questions from clients and performing the searches. Sections on interviewing the client and evaluating client satisfaction are included specifically for the search intermediary. The main focus of the book is on general principles of searching and hands-on experience, which makes the text suitable for those who wish to learn searching for their own use as well. Detailed discussions of search strategy development, databases, vocabulary control, and evaluation of searches have been included, as well as step-by-step instruction in searching techniques. Exercises are included for each of the five chapters that develop searching techniques. The exercises are cumulative; that is, the same search topics are used to illustrate search strategy construction, basic search steps, database selection, and term selection from controlled vocabularies.

The text assumes that the reader will have access to at least one of the three major multi-database commercial retrieval systems: DIALOG Information Services, Inc., System Development Corporation's (SDC) ORBIT system, or Bibliographic Retrieval Services, Inc. (BRS). All of the search examples were run on these systems and the exercises are designed for searching on them. The three systems are discussed generically; mention of specific capabilities is avoided to the extent possible and no attempt is made to compare the systems. The text is designed to be complemented by current system manuals in order to provide the most up-to-date learning materials.

Management aspects of establishing and operating a search service have been excluded from the text, with the exception of a discussion on selecting equipment for the search operation. Academic issues such as the value of information, and policy issues such as client fees, also have been excluded.

The book is compiled specifically as a training text for library school students, practicing librarians, information specialists, and researchers seeking to learn how to use online information retrieval systems. The text is suitable for undergraduate or graduate courses or as a self-teaching handbook in conjunction with system manuals.

Proficiency in searching online retrieval systems requires more than just the reading of one text or the attending of one course. It requires regular practice and experience, along with continued training in new systems, databases, and searching techniques. For these reasons, the text closes with an overview of sources of continuing training in the use of online information retrieval systems.

Christine L. Borgman
Dineh Moghdam
Patti K. Corbett

Acknowledgments

This textbook began with an article for the *Encyclopedia of Library and Information Science* on the topic of "User Training for Online Information Retrieval Systems." That 75-page manuscript became the basis for this text. In the interim, there has been much rewriting, updating, and many contributions by many people.

Much credit must be given to my coauthors, Patti Corbett, who contributed Chapters 5 and 8, and Dineh Moghdam, who contributed Chapters 6 and 7. They have produced excellent material under explicit constraints on time, style, and content, and they endured the extensive revisions necessary to mold the material into a cohesive book.

Appreciation must also be given to the reviewers, who generously donated their time in editing and critiquing the material in draft form. Their efforts have improved the quality of the book and ensured that it is accurate and up-to-date. The reviewers were: George Abbott, Syracuse University; Helen Bell, System Development Corporation; Trudi Bellardo, University of

Kentucky; Jane Bonn, Arapahoe Regional Library; Ted Brandhorst, ERIC Processing and Reference Facility; Elizabeth E. Duncan, University of Pittsburgh; Myra Hodgson, Semiconductor Industry Association; Laura Kassebaum, Bibliographic Retrieval Services; Abby Kratz, University of Texas at Dallas; Tricia McKeown, University of Texas Health Science Center at Dallas; Linda C. Smith, University of Illinois; Bonnie Snow, DIALOG Information Services; Hugh Standifer, Data Services, City of Austin, Texas; and Judith Wanger, Cuadra Associates.

General and specific contributions were made by many others. Thanks must go to the Dallas Public Library, the University of Texas at Dallas Library, and the Stanford University Libraries for the use of materials and resources from their searching operations; to the University of Texas at Dallas, School of Management and Administration, for the use of computer time for text processing; to Carolyn M. Gray of Brandeis University for assistance in the conceptual development of the book and contributions to early drafts; to Carole Bailey and Shirley Nordhaus of UCLA for painstakingly formatting the printouts in Chapters 5 and 8; and to Douglas Ferguson of Research Libraries Group for ideas, encouragement, and use of resources.

Most of my work on this text was done while a doctoral student in the Institute for Communication Research at Stanford University. My academic advisor, William Paisley, and my other colleagues at Stanford and at OCLC (for whom I was working as a research assistant) were most patient while this project diverted my attention from my studies.

Appreciation is also due Allen Kent, at whose urging the Encyclopedia article and this text were written. He has been both a mentor and a friend for many years, and has been patient and supportive throughout this long process.

The greatest single contribution to the effort has come from George M. Mood, who contributed many months of editing, reviewing, and copy preparation, and a wider range of support than can be mentioned here.

Christine L. Borgman
Stanford, California

Contents

EFFECTIVE ONLINE SEARCHING

1

An Overview of Online Information Retrieval Systems

As the amount of published information has grown, traditional methods of storage and retrieval have diminished in effectiveness. At the same time that the problems of this "information explosion" were being recognized, electronic computers were beginning to influence almost every aspect of our lives.

Prior to 1970, however, little public use was made of computerized online information retrieval systems. These systems were in their infancy. They were difficult and expensive to use, and the information available for searching was limited. In just a few years, tremendous increases in both the speed and memory capabilities of computers, along with a dramatic reduction in their cost, made it feasible to store large volumes of information in computerized form. As a result of these technological improvements and the increased availability of computerized data, online information retrieval systems have become a valuable and convenient tool for libraries and information centers.

Online information retrieval systems provide rapid access to a broad range of information at a low cost. Libraries and information centers around the world are finding such systems indispensable to everyday reference services. Several major vendors provide ready access to hundreds of databases containing a wide range of materials. The individual records in some databases may be references to journal articles, technical reports, patents, books, conference papers, annual reports, trade publications, newspaper and magazine articles, standards and specifications, government documents, theses and dissertations, abstracts and bibliographies, and the like. These databases cover most areas of recorded knowledge, and are especially strong in science and technology. Records in other databases may be source data such as economic and financial time series, corporate earnings, chemical properties, laws, survey data, statistics, or any other data that might be retrieved or manipulated (1).

No single library is capable of housing this large volume of material. Even if it could, access would be cumbersome and time consuming. Online systems provide access to this range of information with a minimum of financial investment and a simple but powerful form of access. It is little wonder that these systems are causing major changes in the way libraries collect, retrieve, and disseminate information.

WHAT IS AN ONLINE INFORMATION RETRIEVAL SYSTEM?

An online information retrieval system is a set of computer hardware and computer software for retrieving information from databases. *Computer hardware* is the physical equipment of the computer system, such as the computer itself, various storage devices, and terminals. *Computer software* is the group of programs and procedures that act as instructions to the computer system. A *computer terminal* is a device similar to a typewriter, with a standard keyboard and a few extra keys for communicating with the computer. It includes either a printer or a television-like screen for displaying information, also known as a VDT (video display terminal) or a CRT (cathode ray tube). The terminal sends and receives information to and from the computer over a communication channel such as a telephone line.

As used in this text, *database* refers to a collection of related information that is computer-readable, i.e., capable of being interpreted by a computer system. Databases may be divided roughly into two categories: *bibliographic* (containing references to literature) and *nonbibliographic* (everything else). Bibliographic databases are the computerized equivalent of indexing and abstracting services. Nonbibliographic databases contain source data which may be either numerical or representational in form. The information that describes the document in the database is known as a *document surrogate* or *unit record*. The original data item is called the *document*, and the set of information that can be retrieved from a database is referred to simply as a *record*.

The information retrieval systems discussed in this text are both online and interactive. An *online* system is one in which the user is in direct communication with the computer through a terminal. In an *interactive* system, the user and the computer engage in two-way communication and the response time by the computer is essentially immediate. Interactive systems are also known as *conversational* systems.

THE INFORMATION NETWORK

In one sense, the information retrieval process consists simply of a person sitting at a computer terminal interacting with a computer system. In a larger context, the person and the computer system are components of an information network, or a set of interconnected technologies and organizations. Visualizing the information retrieval process as an information network provides a perspective on how all of the pieces fit together (see Figure 1.1).

When a person searches an information retrieval system, he or she is utilizing a computer terminal, a telecommunications network (usually consisting of telephone lines) for connecting the terminal to the computer, the computer itself, the software or searching programs, and one or more databases. All of these components of the information network are used simultaneously when searching an information retrieval system, yet each of them may be supplied by a different company or organization.

DATABASE PRODUCERS

Database producers are the organizations that collect the information, select appropriate documents or other items for inclusion in the database, and convert the material into computer-readable form. The database producers analyze the documents, extract important information such as the author, title, and source of publication (for bibliographic databases), and may augment the extracted information with additional information such as index terms, abstracts, language codes, or chemical structures.

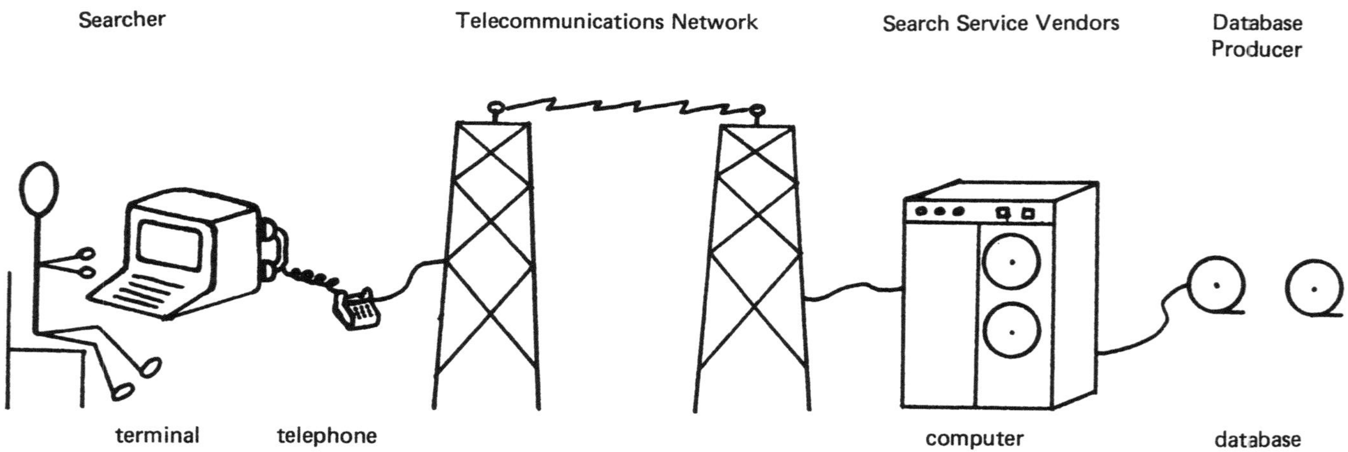

Figure 1.1. An information network.

In the case of bibliographic databases, producers typically subscribe to the journals which are covered by the database, collect other types of literature for inclusion, and index and abstract the materials selected (2). In some cases the selected documents may be both indexed and abstracted; in others they may only be indexed; or they may be neither indexed nor abstracted. For nonbibliographic databases, some indexing or other method of augmenting the records may be required. Conversion to computer-readable form normally requires keying (typing) the records into a computer (e.g., via a terminal) which can convert them to a computerzied format. The records are then stored in mass storage devices such as magnetic tapes or disks (3).

Database producers exist in the public, private, and government sectors of the economy. Public sector database producers are frequently professional societies such as the American Psychological Association or the American Society for Metals. An increasing number of databases are produced by private, for-profit organizations such as the Institute for Scientific Information, Predicasts, Dow Jones, and The New York Times. Government organizations were among the first to generate publicly available databases. There are several prominent government-supported databases such as those produced by the National Library of Medicine and the National Library of Agriculture, and the ERIC (Educational Resources Information Center) database which is produced by several resource centers under government contract.

Many bibliographic databases are the computer-readable counterpart of printed indexing and abstracting services such as ERIC, Psychological Abstracts, and Science Citation Index. Most of the older databases began as "print tapes" used for typesetting the printed versions. More recently, bibliographic databases have been developed that are available only in computer-readable form, with no printed equivalent available for purchase.

In some cases, database producers may also provide computer access to the databases. Typically, however, databases are leased to the organizations that support the computer services and the searching software. These organizations--called search service vendors--usually pay royalty fees to the database producer for the amount of time the database is in use.

SEARCH SERVICE VENDORS

Search service vendors are the organizations that own the computers and the software for information retrieval. These vendors have developed standardized sets of instructions or commands for searching (also known as *search protocol*), as well as software to manipulate the databases.

Vendors either lease databases from database producers or generate their own, in which case they also become database producers. Several large search service vendors lease multiple databases--as many as 100 or more--and make them available with a common search protocol. A number of specialized single database search services are in the market as well. However, as most searching is done through the large systems, they are the primary focus of this text.

Search service vendors usually receive databases from the database producers on magnetic tapes which are then loaded into the vendor's computer system. Processing the tapes includes generating indexes and various access points to the database. The same database may be leased to more than one vendor, in which case there may be differences in the way the data are formatted and the indexes structured, as well as how the database is searched.

Most search service vendors maintain some output or printing capability at the computer site. Users needing a large number of records from a search have the option of printing them at the vendor's computer site (known as *offline printing*) and having them mailed.

The search service computer system has an accounting subsystem which monitors the amount of time that individual terminals and specific searchers are connected to the computer system, how much time is spent searching each database, and the amount of offline printing that is done. All of these items, and perhaps some others, are included in the charges for the use of the search service.

TELECOMMUNICATIONS NETWORKS

Most connections to search service computer systems are made through telecommunications networks known as "value-added networks," or VANs. The two VANs most commonly used on this continent are TYMNET and TELENET, although others are appearing on the market. These networks generally consist of sets of leased telephone lines connected with minicomputers controlling the lines in each major service area. Network access is available on other continents as well.

To use one of the networks, the searcher makes a telephone call to the computer at the nearest access point (or network node) and connects the telephone to the computer terminal. The searcher keys a command into the terminal to identify the terminal to the network and then requests the desired search system. The network makes the link between the terminal and the appropriate computer. Charges for the use of the network are billed by the search service vendor, with a "value added" for the use of the telecommunications network.

THE ROLE OF THE SEARCHER

The final link in the information network is the searcher, who utilizes all of the other components simultaneously. He or she usually accesses the information retrieval system through a computer terminal located in a library or information center. The searcher could also be an executive with a portable terminal in a hotel room, a researcher in a laboratory, or a person searching in any of a wide variety of situations. Since the use of these online information retrieval systems requires a considerable amount of training, most searching is done by specialists employed by libraries or information centers. These specialists perform searches for other persons who have particular information needs or requests. In this text, *searcher, search analyst*, or *search intermediary* refers to the person who actually performs the search and interacts with the information retrieval system. *Client* or *requester* refers to the person making the information request.

The searching process begins with the information need or request. This request is expressed to the searcher, who will structure it into a *search strategy*, a special format that can be understood by the information retrieval system. The searcher determines the appropriate search system and database most likely to satisfy the information need.

The searcher turns the computer terminal on, makes a telephone call to the telecommunications network, and requests the appropriate search system computer. Once the connection to the computer has been made, the searcher requests the desired database. He or she keys the search strategy on the terminal and sends it to the computer. The computer responds with the results of the search (the number of records found or the source data requested). The results may be printed on the terminal, on a printer in the library, or offline at the search service computer site. The searcher also has the option of making changes in the search strategy or choice of databases and of performing additional searches. This process continues until satisfactory results are obtained.

When the search has been finished, the searcher keys a command to exit from the system. This command disconnects the terminal both from the telecommunications network and the search service computer. The searcher hangs up the telephone and turns the terminal off, thus completing the searching process.

HISTORICAL DEVELOPMENT OF ONLINE INFORMATION RETRIEVAL

One of the first uses of computers in the information industry was for typesetting and printing. Indexing and abstracting services, which must sort and compile a vast number of individual records, began to use the computer for production purposes. This was a logical first step in automating information storage, resulting in computer tapes of the indexes and abstracts. Once the information was stored in computer-readable form, it became obvious that other uses could be made of these tapes as well.

When print tapes first became available, computer systems could not yet provide online access at a reasonable cost. Most computer work was processed in batch mode. In a *batch* system, multiple tasks (or in this case, multiple search strategies) are grouped together or "batched" to run through the computer simultaneously. Under the batch method, search questions were entered into the computer via a terminal, magnetic tape, or punched cards (4). Then the questions were matched against the database and the results of all the search strategies were printed at one time. Because the search wasn't performed until enough searches were collected to warrant the computer run, it might be several hours or days (or in the early years, several weeks) before the results of the search were received.

The chief disadvantage of batch searching (besides the delays) is that the search cannot be altered or changed during an interaction with the computer. If the results of the search are not satisfactory, the searcher must alter the search strategy and await the next batch run.

Batch systems were used both for retrospective searches (searching all or part of the previously published literature which is available in the database) and for selective dissemination of information (SDI) searches. An SDI search begins with a continuing information need which is translated into a search strategy. The search is run against one or more databases each time the database is updated (usually monthly or quarterly). This allows an individual user to stay current with new literature as it is published.

In the early days of information retrieval, the major use of retrieval systems was for SDI searches. They are still common, but their use has diminished as interactive searching has become readily available at a reasonable cost. Presently, most searching is retrospective.

The transition from batch systems to online systems was aided both by new computer technologies that lowered computing costs and by the infusion of federal government funds to develop major databases. Lockheed Information Systems and the System Development Corporation (SDC) engaged in independent research to develop computer software to search specific databases online. Government funds were provided to both organizations for database development. The NASA (National Aeronautics and Space Administration), ERIC (Educational Resources Information Center), NTIS (National Technical Information Service), and NAL (National Agricultural Library) databases on DIALOG and the MEDLINE database on SDC were developed through service contracts with the respective agencies.

Those government contracts helped to support the further development of the software packages which serve as a basis for what are now the two largest search service vendors, DIALOG Information Services, Inc., and SDC (ORBIT). The DIALOG search service, formerly known as Lockheed Dialog, is a wholly-owned subsidiary of Lockheed; SDC has now been acquired by the Burroughs Corporation.

The DIALOG system began commercial operation in 1972 with three databases. By 1975, DIALOG had 24 databases; in 1978, over 70; and by 1983, over 170 databases. The SDC ORBIT system begain commercial operation in 1973 with three databases. By 1983, SDC offered more than 70 databases. Over the years, both systems have increased in sophistication and in capabilities offered, and continue to add databases regularly.

The third major system, Bibliographic Retrieval Services (BRS), was a later entry into the market. They began commercial operations in 1977 with nine databases, and by 1983 offered over 70 databases. The system utilizes the IBM STAIRS software which was used by the State University of New York Biomedical Communications Network before BRS was formed. The BRS system also has made regular improvements and continues to add new databases (5).

These three systems account for the majority of database searching performed in libraries and information centers on this continent. Searchers know that it is easier to learn the mechanics of three systems to obtain access to several hundred databases than it is to learn a different set of search protocol for each database to be searched. Once they achieve proficiency in using one or more of these systems, searchers can learn other systems as needed.

Several other search services with more limited database offerings are on the market, and their value should not be overlooked. Examples include The Information Bank, a subsidiary of The New York Times Company (originally known as The New York Times Information Bank and now marketed exclusively by Mead Data) which offers an international database of newspapers and magazines, and the News Retrieval Service of Dow Jones and Company, Inc. Initially these databases were available only as a single database/single search system package. Access to some or all of these databases is now offered by the "big three" as well.

Special purpose systems are also available for certain areas such as law. Lexis and Westlaw, for example, are sophisticated retrieval systems widely used by law libraries and large law firms. These systems are too specialized to cover in an introductory text of this nature. However, information and training on their use is readily available elsewhere.

The information retrieval market has even expanded to home users. For example, DIALOG and BRS now offer database access to anyone with a dial-up terminal or a home computer with communications abilities. Their services are known respectively as "The Knowledge Index" and "BRS/After Hours." Some videotex services, such as The Source and Compuserve, and some two-way cable systems offer online access to databases such as encyclopedias and consumer information. These systems serve a different market and have different training needs, and are not covered in this text.

REFERENCES AND NOTES

1. Hoover, Ryan E. "Overview of Online Information Retrieval." Hoover, Ryan E., ed., *The Library and Information Manager's Guide to Online Services*. White Plains, NY: Knowledge Industry Publications, 1980, p. 1.
2. *Indexing* is the assignment of subject terms, classification numbers, or some other form of standardized identification to a document. *Abstracting* is the creation of a brief summary of the document, usually not more than one or two paragraphs.
3. *Magnetic tape* is tape with a magnetic surface on which data can be stored by selective polarization of portions of the surface. The most common form of magnetic tape for computer applications is a 2400-foot reel of half-inch wide tape. Magnetic tape is also used for sound recording, as in home stereo systems. Tape used for computer applications is of equal or better quality than that used for sound recording. A *disk* is a rotating storage device that provides rapid online access. (DataPhase Systems, *Glossary of Computer Terms*, Rev. Ed., 1979.)
4. A *punched card*, also called a "Hollerith card" after its inventor, Herman Hollerith, is a card in which holes are punched to represent data. It can be read by a machine (a "card reader") for input to a computer. Punched cards typically are 80 columns by 12 rows in size. Each column represents one character (letter, number, or symbol) by punching the appropriate combination of holes in the column.
5. For a more detailed discussion of the history of online services, see: Bourne, Charles P. "On-Line Systems: History, Technology and Economics." *Journal of the American Society for Information Science*, Vol. 31, No. 3 (May, 1980), p. 156-160; and Christian, Roger W. *The Electronic Library: Bibliographic Data Bases, 1978-1979*. White Plains, NY: Knowledge Industry Publications, 1978.

BIBLIOGRAPHY

Bourne, Charles P. "On-Line Systems: History, Technology, and Economics." *Journal of the American Society for Information Science*, Vol. 31, No. 3 (May, 1980), p. 156-160.

Christian, Roger W. *The Electronic Library: Bibliographic Data Bases, 1978-1979.* White Plains, NY: Knowledge Industry Publications, 1978.

Hoover, Ryan E., ed. *The Library and Information Manager's Guide to Online Services.* White Plains, NY: Knowledge Industry Publications, 1980.

Williams, Martha E. "Database and Online Statistics for 1979." *Bulletin of the American Society for Information Science*, Vol. 7, No. 2 (December, 1980), p. 27-29.

2

Characteristics of a Good Searcher

Information retrieval systems are powerful tools but their usefulness is limited by the ability of the searcher to operate them. A good searcher should possess a variety of skills related to online searching, falling roughly into three categories: (1) general principles of searching, which include concepts of information retrieval, gathering information from the client, problem analysis, planning search strategies, evaluation of searches; (2) academic skills, which include subject area knowledge and knowledge of the structure and content of databases, and the use of terminals and telecommunications equipment; and (3) system dependent skills, including connecting to the system and disconnecting, the use of commands or protocol, entry formats for search terms, implementation of logical term relationships on the system, and database implementation.

Searching information retrieval systems requires a combination of technical skills and human communication skills. The searcher must be able to communicate with the client to understand his or her information needs fully. The searcher must also have the technical skills to manipulate the system expertly and retrieve the needed data. The two types of skills complement each other; neither is sufficient alone.

As with any other profession, not all people are suited to be search analysts. This chapter briefly explores some of the individual characteristics that are thought to exemplify the person who can become a good searcher. The suggested characteristics are gathered from a variety of experiential sources; there is no universal agreement on the talents required. The profile of a good searcher is presented to aid the prospective searcher in evaluating his or her own characteristics in terms of the skills required, and to aid the manager who must evaluate or hire search analysts.

HISTORICAL BACKGROUND

When online retrieval systems were first introduced, persons selected and trained to use them came from the ranks of those already trained as librarians or information specialists. Some searchers were selected because of their familiarity with computers or automation in other forms, and some were selected by default as the only staff available. Since then, the systems have been greatly improved, more of them have become available, and their use has vastly increased. Along with these changes came the realization that some special skills are required for online searching in addition to those required for reference librarianship.

PROFILE OF A GOOD SEARCHER

While the following list of traits may not be complete or fully defensible, it serves as a general profile of a person who will perform well as a searcher (1, 2).

Good Communication Skills and a "People" Orientation

Communication and human relations skills are important for successfully interviewing the client and for gathering information about the search request. Such skills enable the searcher to develop an understanding of a problem and to put people at ease.

The searcher must know how to ask open-minded questions and be able to collect both verbal and nonverbal information. Searchers frequently have the responsibility of marketing and promoting the search service, which also requires competent communication skills.

Self Confidence

A searcher should be comfortable with computer terminals and other computer equipment, be dedicated to the job, find it interesting and challenging, and be able to make decisions easily. Searchers must know when searches should and should not be done, and inform the client accordingly. The self-confident searcher is able to convey confidence in the service to the clients.

Patience and Perseverance

Online searching can be a tedious and frustrating experience. It is not always easy to gather the needed information for searching, nor is it always possible to anticipate the results of a search or even to determine the best approach. An online search sometimes can be a trial and error method of seeking information, even for the most experienced of searchers. Online systems and clients are imperfect at best, and the search analyst must be able to judge when to pursue a search further and when it is best to quit.

Logical and Flexible Approach to Problem Solving

Searching requires a logical approach to problem solving. A logically-oriented person typically has an intellectual curiosity and an inquisitive mind, can tolerate ambiguity, and enjoys dealing with cognitive complexity. Such individuals tend to have a common sense approach and are willing to test their own analytical abilities.

A searcher must be able to sort a problem into its component parts, recognizing discrete, overlapping, and unrelated concepts, in order to distinguish between important and extraneous data. An information problem should be examined in more than one perspective simultaneously, recognizing that there may be more than one way to approach it.

Memory For Details

Online searching requires knowledge of such technical aspects as search system mechanics, databases, terminal equipment, and telecommunications protocol. Much of the relevant information is very detailed in nature, such as the precise format for system commands, structure of data elements in individual databases, and telephone numbers for system access. If a searcher uses more than one search system (which is common), the amount of explicit information required is increased accordingly.

Some of the material may be looked up when needed; other details simply must be stored in human memory. The more "online searching facts" that a searcher has at his or her fingertips, the faster the searching will proceed. Speed of searching is critical, since connect time is the basic charge for searching. A searcher who must spend a lot of time looking up forgotten details is not a cost-effective searcher.

Spelling, Grammar, and Typing Skills

Searching a database requires entering terms in the correct form of spelling and grammar usage because the computer can only match letter-by-letter against the terms it has been given. A misspelled word or an unused form of a word will not match against the correct term in the database. A mistyped word will have the same effect if it is not caught and corrected. The searcher must have the skills to spot suspicious terms and verify them for correctness before use in searching.

Subject Area Knowledge

Subject content knowledge in commonly searched topics will aid the searcher in interviewing clients, structuring concepts, and selecting databases. Depending on the type of searching operation, searchers may specialize in one subject area, or be expected to search in a variety of subject areas.

Subject knowledge is particuarly important in specialized areas such as medicine and law. The searcher must have a solid working knowledge of the terminology in these areas to be able to search effectively. In searching operations which handle requests in a wide range of areas, such as public libraries, it may be more useful to be a generalist. Diverse searching operations which are well staffed frequently assign searchers the responsibility for separate subject areas, however.

In either case, a searcher often must become familiar with new subject areas. Skills in reading and scanning material to select essential and non-essential ideas are valuable. Such skills will allow the searcher to become familiar with new subject areas most rapidly.

Good Organization and Efficient Work Habits

Individuals who become good searchers are well organized and have efficient work habits. Online searching requires gathering data about the client's information requirements and about the systems and databases to be searched. All of these data must be analyzed and organized in advance of performing the search. By the time the searcher sits down at a computer terminal to perform the search, the search strategy should be constructed and all pertinent supporting documentation reviewed. Such a sense of organization is necessary to make optimal use of online connect time.

Motivation for Additional Training

In many ways, searching is an art rather than a science, and only the basic skills can be taught through coursework or other forms of training. The searcher must be willing to learn through experience and to pursue additional training as needed. Such additional training may come in many forms, from participation in professional societies or online user groups, to seminars provided by database producers and vendors.

Willingness to Share Knowledge with Others

Most online searching is provided in conjunction with other library reference services. In many libraries and information centers, searchers are part of the regular reference staff and have dual responsibilities. Organizations with a very high searching volume may have separate reference and searching staff. In either case, the searching staff should keep the rest of the staff aware of changes in the search systems, such as new databases offered or significant improvements in searching capabilities. An effective interaction between the reference staff and the searching staff will result in the best utilization of services within the organization.

The searching staff should meet regularly to discuss ideas and problems, and individual searchers must be willing to share new information learned. The professional searcher should participate in outside activities, such as online user groups, where one can share experiences with other searchers and all can gain from the common experience.

SUMMARY

Searching online systems requires a variety of skills and talents. The searcher must be a verbal, communicative person with competent listening skills. He or she should be self-confident, patient and perservering, logical, have a memory for details, possess strong skills in spelling, grammar and typing, and have some subject content knowledge. A good searcher should also be well organized and have efficient work habits, be motivated to obtain additional training, and willing to share this storehouse of training and knowledge with others.

This profile of a searcher may make it appear that only *perfect* individuals can become searchers. Alas, searchers are far from perfect, but they are people with a variety of talents and interests who enjoy the challenge of gaining new knowledge and ideas. It cannot be said too often that an information retrieval system is only as effective as the person who operates it.

REFERENCES AND NOTES

1. Dolan, Donna and Kremin, Michael. "Quality Control of Search Analysts." *ONLINE*, Vol. 3, No. 2 (1979), p. 8-16.
2. van Camp, Ann. "Effective Search Analysts." *ONLINE*, Vol. 3, No. 2 (1979), p. 18-20.

3

Preparing to Search

Computerized information retrieval systems are complex systems that require intensive training and regular use in order to be utilized competently. In the future, online systems will probably be so simple that large scale use by people who are seeking information for themselves (the end users) will be feasible. At present, however, retrieval systems are operated primarily by trained searchers who act as intermediaries between the end user or client and the system itself. The searcher has the responsibility for converting the client's information request into a computer search. This is a difficult process that requires knowledge of both the client's information needs and the search system's capabilities.

This chapter divides the process of search preparation – from the receipt of the search request to the point where the searcher is ready to go online – into three separate topics. First is an introduction to the general principles of structuring an information request in terms suitable for searching; second is a discussion of the types of information requests which are appropriate for searching in an online system; and last is the actual planning of the search.

TRANSLATING THE INFORMATION REQUEST: GENERAL PRINCIPLES

Information retrieval systems are little more than a set of elaborate matching routines performed very quickly on a high-speed computer; the systems cannot "think" in the same manner that humans can. It is not yet possible to sit down at a computer terminal, key a question in the form it is typically asked, and receive an accurate response. Questions such as, "Have there been any pollution problems in the Great Lakes recently?" or, "Is there an antibiotic that will treat toxic shock effectively?" or, "Should the power of the presidency be limited?" cannot be answered directly by the commercially available online information retrieval systems. Computers are capable only of logical, mechanical matching and decision making.

Retrieval systems do not yet have the intelligence capabilities to interpret the language structure or the logical relationships between concepts, or to know the alternative forms of words or synonyms for the phrases given – all of which is done by the human in interpreting such questions. Humans are capable of heuristic problem solving or learning; computers are not.

At the present stage of technological development, it is necessary to translate the information request into a precise, unambiguous statement before the retrieval system can perform the search. The system must be given the exact terminology to be used, frequently including synonyms or alternative forms of the concept, and an explicit statement of the logical relationship between concepts. Given information in this form, the online system can search rapidly through a database, selecting all the items that match the logical statement provided by the searcher.

Those requesting information typically will phrase their question in terms of "Who, what, why, how, . . ." and not in the logical terms required by the retrieval system. It is the searcher's task to take the question as phrased by the client, gather enough information from him or her and from other sources to interpret the question, and then restate it in the terms required by the system. The searcher must be aware that in all but the most highly technical environments, or in cases of frequent use, the client is not likely to understand the needs of the system and therefore is not likely to phrase the question in a readily searchable form. It is the searcher's responsibility to explain the system adequately so that the client will be able to provide any necessary supplemental information. The searcher should also provide the client with realistic expectations of what to expect from the system.

A classic idiom of librarianship is, "a user's access to information is limited by his or her ability to articulate the question." This idiom holds true for access to online systems even more than for traditional forms of information searching. A poorly articulated question often generates an unsatisfactory or incomplete answer. In manual literature searching, the user can browse through the literature and may stumble upon an answer. In searching computerized systems, such browsing is difficult – and expensive. The user or client who has difficulty explaining the information need may still have a valid need for the information. The communication process between the searcher and the client is the channel for gathering enough data to detail the request and eventually provide a well-stated definition of the problem at hand.

DECIDING WHEN TO USE AN ONLINE INFORMATION RETRIEVAL SYSTEM

In most cases, the searcher will hold a "reference interview" with the client to discuss the details of the search request. Part of the interview process will be to determine if the request is one which is best searched through an online system or by more traditional, manual searching methods. The same information can often be found both in printed indexing or abstracting journals and in the computerized database; the difference lies in the form of access.

In order to utilize the capabilities of computerized literature searching to their fullest, searching should be limited to topics with one or more of the following characteristics (1):

1. Searches that require the coordination of two or more distinct concepts; for example, "the effect of vitamin C on the common cold." The two concepts are "vitamin C" and "the common cold."
2. Searches on topics so new or obscure that they may not yet appear as subject headings in printed indexes; for example, gene splicing, or videotex or teletext systems.

3. Searches for information which is known to be more recent than the printed index, and it is known that the online database is current. For example, information on an event occurring within the last month could be searched in databases which are updated daily or even more frequently, such as The Information Bank or the Dow-Jones Retrieval Service.
4. Searches on topics which may be stated in so many synonymous terms that manual searching of indexes would be unreasonably time-consuming. For example, the topic "electron probe microanalysis" is expressible in several different ways, including "X-ray microanalysis" and "microprobe analysis." It would be necessary to search under all three of these phrases in a printed index.
5. Searches which are relatively narrow in scope and are likely to result in rather small retrieval. For example, in a search of the Chemical Abstracts database, the topic "pesticide residues in food" may retrieve 700 or more references. It may be more appropriate to consult a book or journal review article on this broad topic than to print out such a large number of references. A more appropriate search would be for the latest references on this topic (limit the search by date of publication) or for a limited portion of the topic, such as "DDT residues in milk" or "pesticide residues in mother's milk."
6. Topics covered in databases that do not have a corresponding printed index. While many databases include information which duplicates printed indexes, some databases have no printed counterpart. If this is the case, and the database is the most appropriate source of information, the topic should be searched in the database even if the other rules do not apply.

Searches Which May Not Be Appropriate for Database Searching

Several types of searches may not be suitable for database searching, and may be difficult to search manually as well. They may be unsuccessful due to the way in which the question is asked, the subject of the search, the indexing of databases (or the lack of indexing), the information retrieval system which supports the database, or some combination of the above. As changes are made in the indexing of databases, as databases in new subjects are made available, and as changes are made in the way databases are loaded onto search systems, the types of questions which are appropriate will change.

It is important for the searcher to be aware of questions which will not provide good search results. It is better to forewarn the client of potential problems than to present unreasonable expectations. Some examples of types of questions which are likely to cause problems, either because of the subject area or the way in which the question is phrased, are listed below (2).

Hypothetical Questions. "What if?" questions generally are difficult to search in databases. An example would be, "If a cure for cancer were found, what would be the effect on the economy?" There is not much written directly on such topics; at best, one might find articles which discuss the hypothetical questions as one of several topics in an article. Finding such articles is limited by the depth and type of indexing.

Practical, Ethical or Moral Questions. Expository questions, such as "What do I do if . . .," are rarely covered in research-oriented databases. A similar problem occurs with ethical or moral questions, such as those concerning prison reform, limiting the powers of the presidency, alcoholism among attorneys, and so on. Both of these types of questions might be searched best in a newspaper or magazine database or index.

Ranges or Comparisons. Any question requiring a concept such as "degrees of . . .," "comparisons between . . .," or quantity or quality is difficult to search. The indexing rarely supports this type of question unless the question is rephrased significantly.

Interdisciplinary Questions. Interdisciplinary questions can be searched in databases, but are difficult to do well. They are included here because the results may not be satisfactory and the problems should be discussed with the client.

Some interdisciplinary questions cross too many disciplinary boundaries to search in any single-subject-oriented databases. One of the best ways to search these questions is to divide them into subject-related parts and search the parts separately, each in the most appropriate database for that aspect of the question. Multidisciplinary databases, such as SciSearch (Science Citation Index) and Social SciSearch (Social Science Citation Index), are also useful for questions that do not fall clearly into one subject area.

Topics Outside the Scope of Available Databases

Online databases are not available for every subject area covered in a major public or academic research library. Databases exist for material which is used frequently enough in proportion to its volume to justify the costs of putting it in computer-readable form and making it searchable. Science and technology have the most database coverage, followed by business and economics and the social sciences; far less coverage is available for history and the humanities. Some subject areas, such as ancient history, are rarely covered by databases.

PLANNING THE SEARCH

Search planning starts with the receipt of the client's search request and includes the steps up to the actual conduct of the online search. In this section, various aspects of the reference interview and final preparations for the search are discussed.

The Reference Interview

The purpose of the reference interview is to obtain enough information from the client to search the retrieval system effectively. To accomplish this, the searcher must be able to communicate well with the client.

The starting point for discussion in the reference interview is the client's written information request. The request is generally written on a standard form provided for this purpose, either prior to the interview or at the beginning of it. The form aids the clients in defining their information needs, and helps the searcher to understand those needs as well. Sample search request forms are shown in Figures 3.1 and 3.2.

The second step in the process is usually a face-to-face interview between the searcher and the client. If a written form has not been used, comparable information will be gathered during the interview. In some cases, the searcher may do some preliminary work on the search request between the time that the written request is made and the interview occurs. Such preliminary work will often be necessary if the search is in a subject area unfamiliar to the searcher.

The list of topics to be covered in the reference interview will vary, based on such factors as the searcher's familiarity with

STANFORD UNIVERSITY LIBRARIES
COMPUTER SEARCH SERVICE

ONLINE SEARCH REQUEST FORM

Client's Name ________________________________ Date ____________________

SEARCH TOPIC: Describe the subject/topic you want searched in one or more clear and precise statements. Here are two examples: (1) "The effects of any mutation on the eye color of the fruit fly (Drosophila melanogaster)." (2) "How importing steel has affected the U.S. economy."

____

____

KEYWORDS: Use the back of this form to list key terms, phrases or concepts that describe the topic you want searched.

SAMPLE CITATIONS: List 2 or 3 bibliographic citations (author, title, pagination, etc.) on your topic, if known or easily available.

____

____

____

LANGUAGES: ___English only. ___Any language. Languages in addition to English __________

____

RANGE OF YEARS WANTED: ___All years available. ___Nothing before 19___, after 19___.

ABSTRACTS (i.e. summaries of material retrieved) DESIRED (if available): ___Yes. ___ No.

SCOPE OF SEARCH: Check the kind of search you want conducted.

_____Comprehensive: Attempt to retrieve the maximum amount of related material even if much of it is not precisely on target.

_____Very Precise: Attempt to retrieve a limited amount of highly relevant material even if more general, related material is not retrieved.

FEE LIMIT: The approximate amount acceptable as a maximum fee. $____________________.
Note: The search must be paid for even if relevant material is not found.

DEADLINE: Search results will not be useful after ____________________________(date).

SURVEY QUESTION: How did you hear about this service? ___Library Staff.
___Library Demonstration. ___Poster/Flyer. ___Newspaper Ad. ___Instructor.
___Friend/Colleague. ___Other (please specify)____________________________________.

AUTHORIZATION: I authorize the library staff to perform this search and agree to pay the charges incurred by: ___Check, ___Money Order, ___Interdepartmental fund transfer, or ___Cash.

Signature: ____ Date____________________

1/21/81 ***OVER***

Figure 3.1. Search request form. (Used by permission of Stanford University.)

Return completed request form to
LIBRARIAN
Graduate School of Public Health
University of Pittsburgh
Pittsburgh, Pennsylvania 15261

COMPUTERIZED BIBLIOGRAPHIC SEARCH REQUEST

Date

Name of individual requesting search Last First Middle	Telephone *(Please include area code)* Business: Home:
Institution or organization with which affiliated	Status/position *(Please include department)*

Mailing address: P.O. Box and/or Street, City, State and Zip Code

PITT USE ONLY: charge to University account number__________________
DETAILED STATEMENT OF SEARCH REQUIREMENTS: *Please explain in sentence form the specific information desired.*

PURPOSE OF SEARCH

☐ Lecture ☐ Paper ☐ Patient Care ☐ Research

☐ Other ____________________________

PLEASE COMPLETE OTHER SIDE.

Figure 3.2. Search request form. (Used by permission of the Graduate School of Public Health Library, University of Pittsburgh.)

MOST RECENT OR MOST RELEVANT ARTICLES READ ON THE SUBJECT *(If you have carried out a preliminary literature search, please supply full bibliographical citations below. These citations will be used as a guide in retrieving citations related to your needs.)*

If you used INDEX MEDICUS for your preliminary search, please list the subject headings under which you found citations.

LIMITATIONS FOR SEARCH *(Check those which apply.)*

☐ English Language Only
☐ All Languages
☐ Other Languages (please
☐ specify): ____________

☐ Male
☐ Female
☐ No Restrictions

☐ Human Subjects
☐ Animal Experiments
☐ No Restrictions

☐ Review Articles Only
(State of Art)

Age Groups (MEDLINE only)

☐ No Restrictions
☐ Pregnancy
☐ Infant, Newborn (to 1 month
☐ Infant (1-23 months)
☐ Child, Preschool (2-5 years)
☐ Child (6-12 years)
☐ Adolescence (13-18 years)
☐ Adult (19-44 years)
☐ Middle Age (45-64 years)
☐ Aged (65 years and up)

DATA BASES TO BE SEARCH:
(This section to be filled in by Librarian.)

Please do not write below this line.

Date search received	Search analyst	Date search released

Search statement

Figure 3.2. (Continued)

the subject area and appropriate databases, the client's familiarity with online searching, the depth and breadth of the search requested, and the types of restrictions the client chooses to place on the search. For the searcher, the end result of the reference interview should be an understanding of the search request. For the client, the result of the reference interview should be a reasonable understanding of how the system works and what may be expected from it.

Topics to Cover in the Reference Interview

The following is a list of general guidelines for the reference interview (3). In some interviews it may be necessary to cover all the points thoroughly; in others some points may be glossed over or skipped entirely if the client is already familiar with them. The order of discussion may vary as well. Each of these topics is discussed in greater detail in subsequent chapters.

1. *Discuss the uses and benefits of online searching.* The searcher should briefly discuss some of the reasons for using online information retrieval systems and the cases in which they are most appropriate, and should point out the advantages over manual searches of the literature, such as searching multiple access points, logically combining topics, and the interactive capabilities of changing the search while online. The limitations of online searching should also be discussed, such as the limited period of coverage of some databases, and the letter-for-letter matching which may not pick up related or component terms that are spelled differently.
2. *Discuss the types of questions for which computer searching is appropriate.* It should be determined early in the interview if the request is appropriate for a computer search, based on the criteria suggested above. If not, the question should be referred back to the regular reference services.
3. *Discuss the subject with the client.* It is important for the searcher to know something about the topic, both to understand the topic and the terminology and to gain credibility with the client. If the searcher is not comfortable working in the subject area, more outside reading should be done before performing the search.
4. *Understand the question.* The search analyst should understand the question well enough to sort out the different concepts and the relationships between them. This requires a more detailed understanding than simply being able to follow the question as asked.

5. *Discuss the scope of the information request.* The searcher must know how comprehensive the search is to be and structure it accordingly. For example, is this going to be an "everything ever published" search for a doctoral dissertation or a research and development project? Does it require only a few important citations, such as for a high school or college freshman term paper? Should the search pick up only the most recent articles, as for a scholar who is working in the field and wants only an update?
   The searcher should discuss any other limits to be placed on the search, such as geographical (e.g., U.S. materials only), language (e.g., English and German language articles only), or date (e.g., most recent year only, or last five years). Specific limitations vary by database and search system.
6. *Develop the search strategy.* Developing a search strategy is the process of stating the information request in precise terms, specifying the logical relationship of concepts and the exact terminology to be used. Frequently, more than one search strategy should be developed in case the first one does not achieve the desired results.
   Specifying the logical relationship between terms requires the use of Boolean logic, which is discussed in the next chapter along with the details of forming a search strategy. Specifying the exact terminology may require a thesaurus, or standard list of terms for indexing a particular database. This is discussed in Chapter 7.
   The final form of the search strategy will depend upon the database selected, because of differences in types of material and formatting as well as differences in terminology. The concepts and relationships between them must be established in order to select the database, however. For this reason, the search strategy should be outlined before the database is selected.
7. *Describe the appropriate databases.* Briefly describe the databases suitable for the particular search, including format, content, and degree of overlap between the databases. The client should understand that some databases may contain only a brief citation – such as author, title, and source of material – while others may contain index terms, abstracts, and other supplemental information. If the library or organization owns the printed counterpart of the database, such as Psychological Abstracts, Chemical Abstracts, or ERIC (Educational Resources Information Center), it may be useful to make comparisons to the printed copy.

Coverage of the database should be discussed, both as to the material included and the years of coverage. While some printed indexes may go back decades, the online database may cover only a few years. An increasing number of databases do not have printed counterparts; where this is the case, the online database may be the only access point to the desired information.

Clients sometimes suggest the database they wish to use, and the searcher should discuss this with them. Some clients may be very familiar with the literature of their field and know where the information is most likely to be found. Others, particularly those unfamiliar with retrieval systems and library techniques, may suggest a database on hearsay alone. For example, someone may have told the client that an ERIC search is useful, yet this person's topic falls in engineering, which is far outside the scope of the ERIC database. Explain the relative merits of the databases and which database is most appropriate and why.

8. *Discuss costs of the search.* In most organizations, the client will be charged for the costs of the online search. Therefore, the client should understand the charging structure and relative costs of performing the search in different ways. The costs of time spent in online searching relative to the costs of offline printing of citations should be discussed, for example. Records are usually printed offline, which is less expensive than online printing but requires a delay of several days before the output is received by mail. If the client requires the output immediately, a premium must be paid for the online printing.

   Another consideration is the amount of online time to spend refining the search. While the cost of offline printing may be high, it is sometimes less expensive to print a few unnecessary references offline than to spend the online time refining the search to the point that all citations are highly relevant to the information request.
9. *Describe software features and their usage.* Software capabilities vary somewhat between online information retrieval systems. If there are distinctions between systems which apply to the search, it may be useful to discuss them with the client. Only a brief description is generally necessary. Some clients may be interested in discussing software; most will not.

   Software features are not discussed in detail in this text since they are system-specific and subject to frequent change.

As the searcher becomes familiar with individual systems through using them, reading system documentation, and attending vendor-sponsored training sessions, greater knowledge of the software will develop.

10. *Perform a final check.* Before closing the interview, the searcher should make sure the information gathered is complete. The vocabulary should be established, along with synonyms and alternative terms so the searcher can make any necessary changes at the terminal. If the client has done any literature searching of the topic already, the searcher should be told what the citations are, as well as any authors or companies known to be working in the field, since that information may be useful in the search. The searcher should also know what deadlines apply to the request; information that arrives after it is needed may be of little or no value.

Hold a Second Interview If Necessary

Sometimes two meetings between the searcher and the client may be required before the search is performed. After the first meeting, the searcher might do some background reading to become more familiar with the topic and the terminology. The final meeting would be to pin down the exact terms and strategy to be used in the search.

Final Preparations for the Search

After the reference interview is completed, it is frequently necessary to perform several other tasks before going to the terminal. If the client will be present during the search, it may be appropriate for him or her simply to wait while the other tasks are performed. Or it may be preferable to schedule the search for a later time if a lot of additional work remains. Search scheduling is only a problem if the client is planning to be present at the time of the search.

Some searching operations have a policy of not doing searches with the client present, in which case a group of searches can be run at once, saving both staff time and computer connect time. The advantage of having the client present is that relevance judgements can be made as references are retrieved, and the search strategy can be adjusted readily to the client's needs. The disadvantages are that the search frequently takes longer (and thus is more expensive) and requires more complex scheduling of search and staff time.

The next task is to determine exactly which databases are to be searched. If the search is a simple one, and the applicable databases are well known to the searcher, this may have been decided in the reference interview. Such a large number of databases are available that it frequently is not feasible to make that decision without examining the directories of databases. This involves reviewing database descriptions in the user manuals and other sources, and may require examining the printed index equivalents of the databases under consideration.

The online search service may also provide an online *database of databases*, a subject-searchable index to the contents of databases available on the search system. All three of the major search vendors (DIALOG, SDC, and BRS) currently provide such a database.

Once the appropriate database has been selected, the searcher should use the vocabulary aids available for the database in making the final choice of terms for the search. If the suitability of certain terms is not clear, a quick manual search through any corresponding printed indexes may be helpful.

The last step in planning the search is to finalize the search strategy. Search strategy construction is the topic of the next chapter.

SUMMARY

Information retrieval systems are complex and, at the present state of development, require operation by specially trained searchers who act as intermediaries between the client and the search system. It is the searcher's responsibility to convert the client's information need into a precise search statement that can be operated upon by the system. To do this, the searcher must understand both the information request and the system capabilities.

Not all search requests are appropriate for computerized searching. The searcher must be able to distinguish between those requests that are searchable and those that are not, and handle the request accordingly.

The searcher interviews the client to gather information about the scope and purpose of the request, and may need to check other sources to aid in defining the request. Part of the interview involves explaining the system's capabilities to the client. This aids the client in supplying appropriate information about the request and creates a realistic level of expectation about results from the search.

The searcher utilizes the data gathered from the reference interview and other sources to create a statement of the search and select the appropriate database(s). The searcher then performs the search online, with or without the client present.

REFERENCES AND NOTES

1. The criteria for determining topics appropriate for searching is based on training materials developed for the Amigos Bibliographic Council, Dallas, Texas, by Carolyn M. Gray.
2. Dolan, Donna R. "OFFLINES: What Databases Cannot Do." *DATABASE*, Vol. 2, No. 3 (1979), p. 85-87.
3. Somerville, Arlene. "The Place of the Reference Interview in Computer Searching: The Academic Setting." *ONLINE*, Vol. 1, No. 4 (1977), p. 14-27.

BIBLIOGRAPHY

Dolan, Donna R. "OFFLINES: What Databases Cannot Do." *DATABASE*, Vol. 2, No. 3 (1979), p. 85-87.

Somerville, Arlene. "The Place of the Reference Interview in Computer Searching: The Academic Setting." *ONLINE*, Vol. 1, No. 4 (1977), p. 14-27.

4

Search Strategy Construction

As mentioned previously, none but the most sophisticated of the experimental information retrieval systems can accept a question in the way it is normally asked and interpret it well enough to provide a proper answer. At present, the searcher must translate the search request into a standardized format upon which the system can operate. This format is called a *search strategy*, although it is sometimes referred to as a *search statement* or *search profile* or just *profile*. The search strategy accomplishes two objectives: it explicitly states the concepts in the information request, and explicitly states the relationship between those concepts.

This chapter discusses search strategy construction in general terms, independent of search system-specific requirements, in order to provide an understanding of the principles involved. Specific forms of entering a search strategy into the retrieval system are discussed in subsequent chapters.

TRANSLATING THE INFORMATION NEED

Search strategy construction begins with the client's information need or search request. The first step is to examine the request and identify the concepts that are stated in it. An example of a simple search request might be, "I'm looking for some information about the United Nations." This request has only one concept: "United Nations."

It is more common to find search questions with more than one concept. An example would be, "I need current information on research about the effects of vitamin C on the common cold." This question contains two concepts: "vitamin C" and "common cold." Another example of a multiple concept search request is, "We would like some recent data on prime interest rates and also on home mortgage rates." This also contains two concepts: "prime interest rates" and "home mortgage rates."

The second step in search strategy construction is to identify the relationship between the concepts. In the first request there is only one concept: "United Nations." In such a case, all references containing mention of the United Nations is sought, and no relation to any other concept is implied. In the second question, about vitamin C and the common cold, the client is seeking references which contain information on *both* concepts. Articles containing information on vitamin C but not the common cold and articles containing information about the common cold but not about vitamin C are not acceptable results for this search request. By requiring *both* concepts to appear in the same article, an *AND* relationship between the two concepts is created.

The third request, about prime interest rates and home mortgage rates, is a multiple concept question but not an AND question. The requester desires any information about either prime interest rates or home mortgage rates, but not restricted to articles which contain information on both concepts simultaneously. This is known as an *OR* relationship between the concepts. Articles about prime interest rates OR articles about home mortgage rates will satisfy this search request.

BOOLEAN LOGIC

The relationships AND and OR are logical connectors from a system known as *Boolean logic*. The system is named after George Boole, the mathematician who invented it. Boolean logic is a combinatorial system that represents symbolically the relationships between sets or concepts. In the above examples, the relationship between concepts was stated in narrative form (e.g., vitamin C AND the common cold); it is also useful to examine the relationships in pictorial form.

Simple Boolean Statements

A single concept search request such as, "Please find some information about the United Nations" becomes a simple search strategy:

United Nations

Only references containing this term will be retrieved from the database being searched. The results of the search strategy can be shown pictorially as in Figure 4.1.

The box represents the database being searched and the circle represents all of the references which contain the term "United Nations." The shaded area represents the references which would be retrieved from the database.

The second question, about vitamin C and the common cold, becomes a slightly more complex search strategy:

vitamin C AND common cold

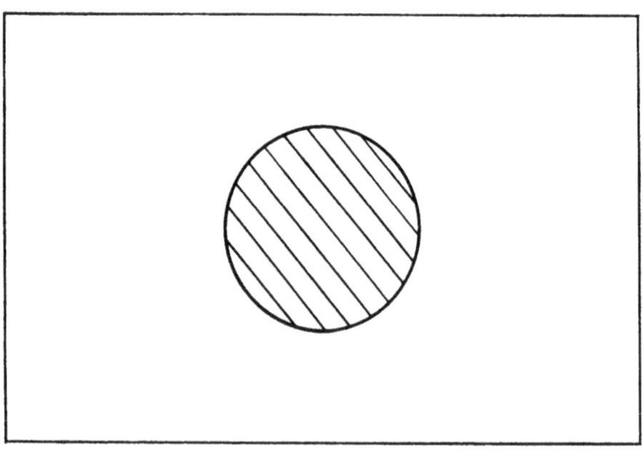

Figure 4.1.

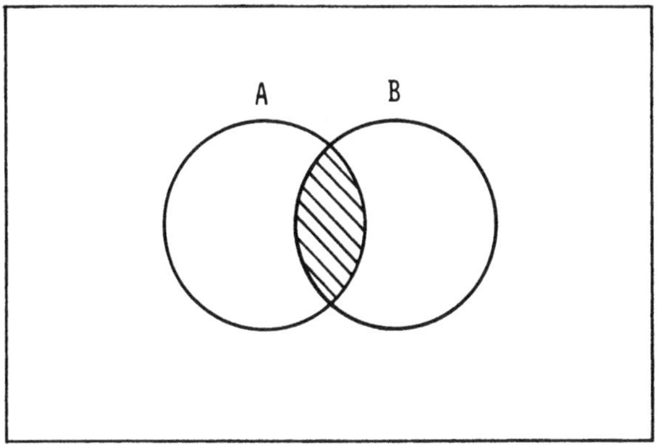

Figure 4.2.

This search strategy will retrieve only references from the database which contain both the term "vitamin C" and the term "common cold." This AND search strategy can be represented pictorially as in Figure 4.2.

The box represents the database being searched, circle A represents the set of all references containing the term "vitamin C," circle B represents the set of all references containing the term "common cold," and the shaded area represents the desired references which contain both concepts.

The third question, about prime interest rates and home mortgage rates, becomes the following search strategy:

prime interest rates OR home mortgage rates

This OR strategy can be represented pictorially as follows in Figure 4.3.

The box represents the database being searched, circle A represents the set of all references containing the term "prime interest rates," circle B represents the set of all references containing the term "home mortgage rates," and the shaded areas represent the desired references which contain either or both concepts.

Notice that the OR logical connector (also called *logical operator*) will retrieve references contained in either of the two sets it connects, plus references which are in both sets (those which an AND would retrieve). The OR logical connector used

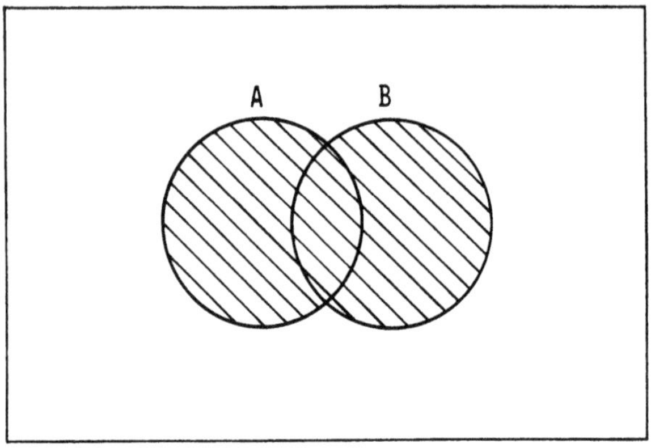

Figure 4.3.

by most retrieval systems (and all of the most commonly used commercial systems) is an *inclusive OR* which retrieves all items in each set plus those which are in the intersection of the two sets. The alternative to an inclusive OR is an *exclusive OR* which retrieves items contained in either of the two sets combined by OR but does not retrieve items which are found in the intersection of the two sets, as shown below in Figure 4.4.

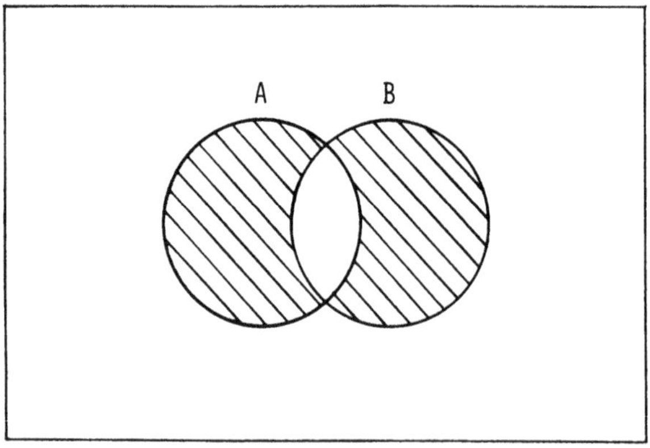

Figure 4.4.

This distinction should be noted, as some systems may provide an exclusive OR as an option, although the normal use of OR can be assumed to be an inclusive OR.

Another Boolean logic connector exists for the purpose of excluding items from a set; this is the *AND NOT* operator. (In some systems it may be *NOT* or *BUT NOT*.) It is useful in search requests such as, "I would like information about water pollution, but not about water pollution in the Great Lakes." This request has two concepts: "Water pollution" and "Great Lakes." The requester wants references which contain the term "water pollution," but only if they do not also contain the term "Great Lakes." This results in the following search strategy:

water pollution AND NOT Great Lakes

The search strategy can be represented by the following diagram, Figure 4.5.

The box represents the database being searched, circle A represents the set of all references containing the term "water pollution," circle B represents the set of all references containing the term "Great Lakes," and the shaded area represents the desired references which contain only the "water pollution" term.

The searcher is advised to apply the AND NOT operator cautiously, as it will eliminate any references containing the excluded term even if all other criteria in the search strategy are

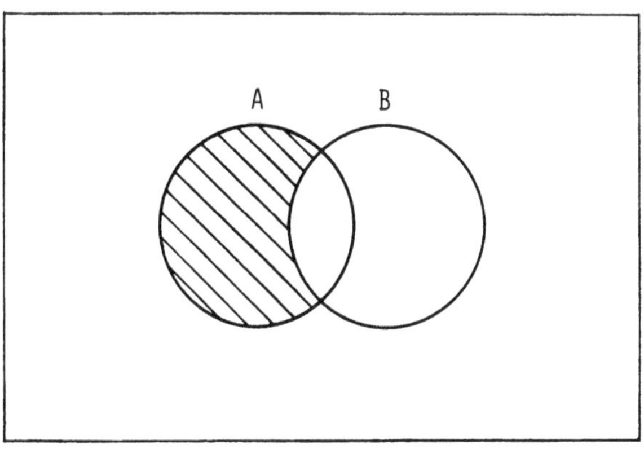

Figure 4.5.

met. In the previous search strategy, for example, a document which covers "water pollution" comprehensively but also mentions "Great Lakes" would be eliminated from the retrieved results.

Using Multiple Logical Connectors

The preceding examples of search strategy construction have used only one logical connector and one term to represent each concept. Search strategies frequently contain more than one logical operator and use more than one term to represent a single concept. Search statements which have too many terms and relationships to be expressed by only one logical operator can be made into compound search statements using as many operators as necessary.

Operators can be repeated in a search statement (e.g., "the United Nations OR North Atlantic Treaty Organization OR World Health Organization") and mixed where necessary (e.g., "vitamin C AND common cold OR influenza"). Most systems have technical limits on the number of terms and operators that can be used in a search strategy, but the limits are high enough (25 terms or more) not to impose practical limits. Compound search strategies are frequently entered into the system in steps rather than all at once, making it easier to keep track of how each part of the strategy expands or restricts the search.

An example of a multiple concept search request might be, "I need some information for a term paper on stereotypes of women in the mass media." The request has three concepts: "stereotypes," "women," and "mass media." This is another example of an AND relationship, but between all three concepts. Only references which are about stereotypes AND about women AND about mass media will satisfy this search request. Thus, the search strategy for this question would be as follows:

stereotypes AND women AND mass media

This multiple AND search strategy can be represented by the following diagram, Figure 4.6.

The box represents the database being searched, circle A represents the set of all references containing the term "stereotypes," circle B represents the set of all references containing the term "women," circle C represents the set of all references containing the term "mass media," and the shaded area represents the desired set of references which contain all three concepts.

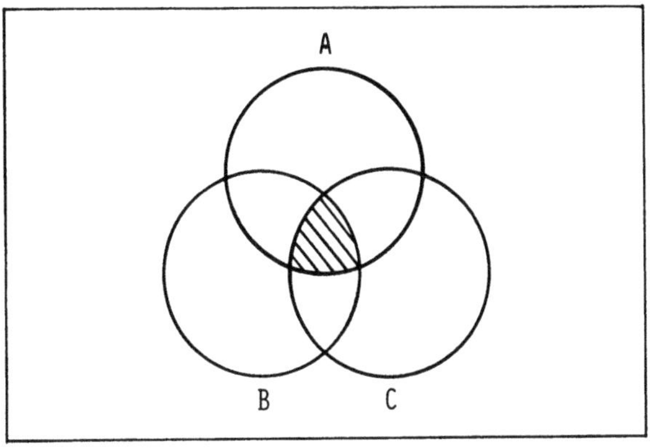

Figure 4.6.

Another search request requiring multiple logical connectors would be, "I need information about water pollution in the Great Lakes, but I don't want anything about Lake Erie." This request has three concepts: "water pollution," "Great Lakes," and "Lake Erie."

The AND operator can be used to connect "water pollution" and "Great Lakes" and the AND NOT operator can be used to exclude "Lake Erie." The following search strategy would result:

pollution AND Great Lakes AND NOT Lake Erie

This compound search strategy can be represented pictorially as follows in Figure 4.7.

The box represents the database being searched, circle A represents the set of all references containing the term "water pollution," circle B represents the set of all references containing the term "Great Lakes," and circle C represents the set of all references containing the term "Lake Erie." The shaded area represents the set of all references which would be retrieved by this search strategy.

A common form of search request is one which requires several concepts to be connected to each other by OR and these in turn connected to some other concept by AND. For example, "Please find some information about the effect of federal government regulations on prime interest rates or on home mortgage rates." The three concepts in this question are: "federal gov-

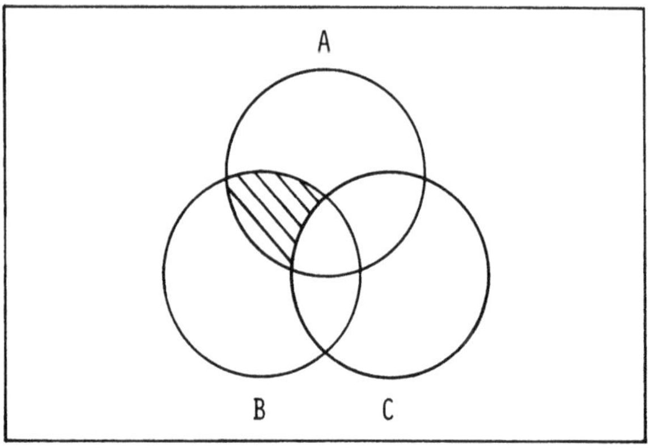

Figure 4.7.

ernment regulations," "prime interest rates," and "home mortgage rates." The following search strategy would result:

federal government regulations
AND
(prime interest rates OR home mortgage rates)

The parentheses are used to clarify the relationship between the terms.

The following diagram, Figure 4.8, represents this search strategy.

Circle A represents "federal government regulations," circle B represents "prime interest rates," and circle C represents "home mortgage rates."

An even more complex search question might be, "Please locate information about police or law enforcement activities in Baltimore, New York, or Chicago." The search strategy for this question would be as follows:

(police OR law enforcement)
AND
(Baltimore OR New York OR Chicago)

The diagram for this strategy is shown in Figure 4.9.

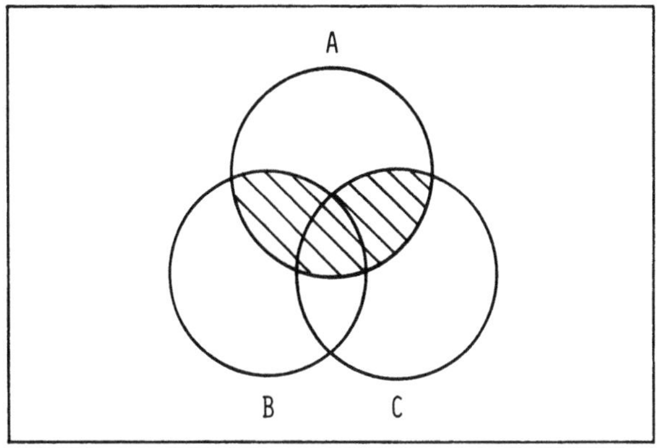

Figure 4.8.

Circle A represents "police," circle B represents "law enforcement," circle C represents "Baltimore," circle D represents "New York," and circle E represents "Chicago."

As more terms and more connectors are used, the diagrams become more complicated. They can be simplified by examining some of the relationships within the search strategy. When terms

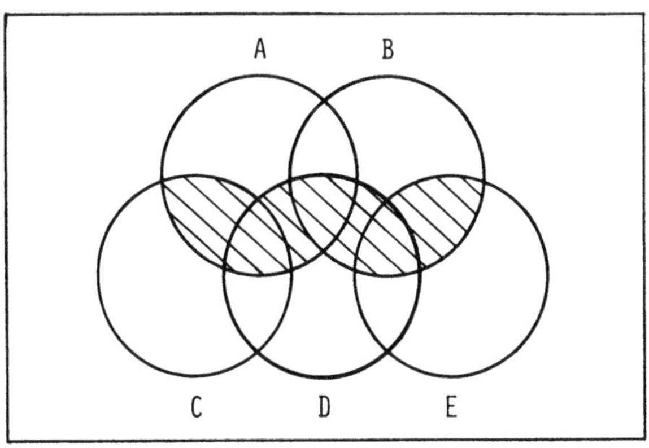

Figure 4.9.

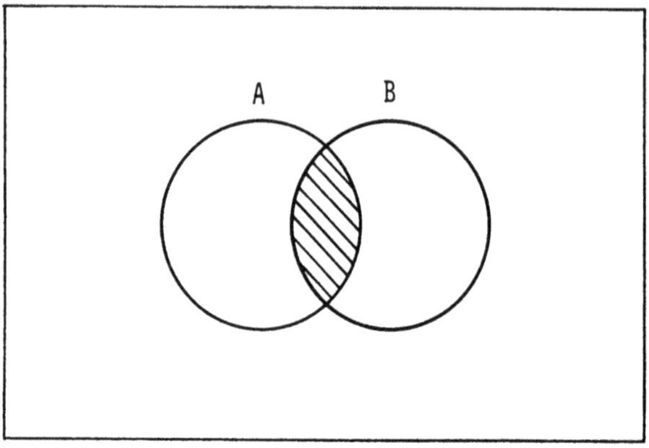

Figure 4.10.

are connected by an OR, all references containing either or both terms are retrieved. Thus, it is possible to think of the terms combined by OR as a single set, all of which will be treated as equivalent in the search strategy. Thinking of "police OR law enforcement" as one set and "Baltimore OR New York OR Chicago" as another set, the search strategy can be represented as a simple AND strategy (Figure 4.10).

This diagram also clarifies the results of the search. References retrieved will contain either the term "police" or the term "law enforcement" or both terms, and also will contain one or more of the terms "Baltimore," "New York," or "Chicago."

Using Multiple Terms for a Single Concept

The previous examples have used one term to represent each concept for the purpose of clarity in explanation. In actual practice it is often advisable to represent a single concept with multiple terms, particularly when doing a subject search. The searcher can create a list of synonyms or alternative terms which may have been used to describe the desired concept. Authors or indexers frequently apply descriptive terms that are different from those which may first come to the searcher's mind. Using multiple terms for a concept increases the likelihood of retrieving the desired material from the database.

When building a search strategy, it is important to understand that a computer does not search for "concepts" but only matches the terms it has been given against the terms found in the database on a word-for-word and even a letter-by-letter basis. Therefore, if the search strategy has used the term "vitamin C" and the concept has been stored in the database as "ascorbic acid," no match will be found. The concepts are identical, but the letter-by-letter match of the terms is not.

In discussing the inclusion of alternative search terms, it is helpful to understand the difference between "controlled" and "uncontrolled" vocabulary in a database. In a controlled vocabulary database, a standardized list has been used in entering all subject terms. The list of subject terms is called a "thesaurus," and normally is available either as a bound book or as a set of microfiche or is stored online with the database in the retrieval system.

The controlled vocabulary standardizes or "controls" the use of terms. Decisions are made about the terms that will be used to describe a concept, and then all occurrences of that concept are described with the chosen term. For example, the term "vitamin C" may be chosen to represent the concept "vitamin C/ ascorbic acid." The searcher can consult the thesaurus to find out which term has been chosen, and then use only that term to represent the concept. It is not necessary to enter the synonym because it has not been used as a subject term in that particular database.

In an uncontrolled vocabulary database, no such standardization has been done. The subject terms available for matching may be those used by each individual author or indexer. In this case it is important to use all synonyms or alternative terms that may be appropriate. The use of controlled and uncontrolled vocabulary databases is discussed in more detail in Chapters 7 and 8.

A single request frequently may be searched in more than one database. Due to differences in vocabulary terms between databases, it may be necessary to use different forms of the strategy in searching each database. Databases also differ greatly in type of material contained, in focus, and in format. The search strategy must be tailored to the database, and thus cannot be finalized until the databases have been selected.

Exhibit 4.1 contains lists of search terms which might be used to describe a given topic. Synonyms or alternative terms for a concept are combined in a search strategy by using the OR connector. The concept "vitamin C/ascorbic acid," for example, may be described by the following phrase:

vitamin C OR ascorbic acid

The phrase can then be used alone as a search strategy or in combination with another search term or phrase. To return to the earlier example of "vitamin C AND common cold," synonyms and related terms for "common cold" can be added to form the following search strategy:

(vitamin C OR ascorbic acid)
AND
(common cold OR influenza OR flu)

By considering each group of terms combined by OR as a single set, the search strategy can be shown pictorially as follows in Figure 4.11.

Circle A represents the concept "vitamin C OR ascorbic acid," and circle B represents the concept "common cold OR influenza OR flu."

The three concept search strategy, "women AND stereotypes AND mass media" can be expanded similarly. The following search strategy might result:

(women OR females OR feminism)
AND
(stereotypes OR sex roles)
AND
(mass media OR television OR radio OR movies)

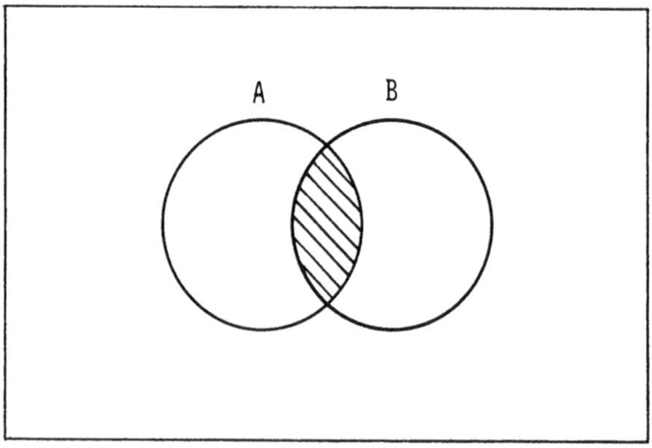

Figure 4.11.

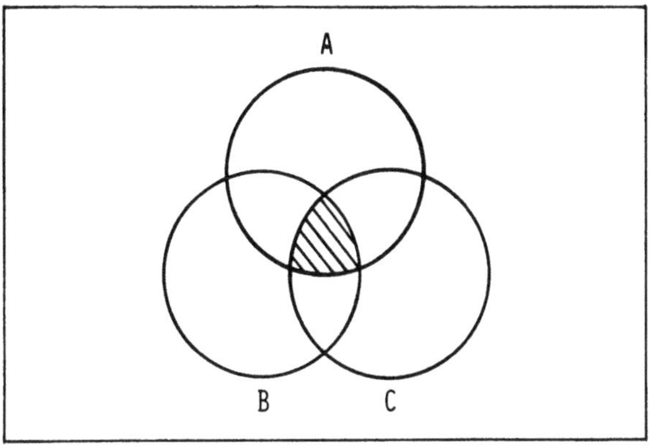

Figure 4.12.

This strategy can be diagrammed as shown in Figure 4.12.
Circle A represents the concept "women OR females OR feminism," circle B represents the concept "stereotypes OR sex roles," and circle C represents the concept "mass media OR television OR radio OR movies."

SUMMARY

For simplicity in introducing the principles of search strategy construction, the examples of terms have been simple subjects, names, or places. A variety of other types of terms can be used in a search strategy, such as author names, geographical areas, chemical structures, dates, or language of publication, which vary by the particular database and the information retrieval system selected.

The examples of search questions used in this chapter have been kept simple so that the concepts and relationships between them may be extracted easily. Such simplicity is rarely the case in questions that will be searched in a full scale searching operation. Because of the difficulties in precisely defining concepts and picking appropriate terms for searching a question in a particular database, there is rarely only one "right" search strategy. In fact, the most successful searcher is probably one who can look at a complex search request in more than one way and come up with two or more search strategies. This approach is particularly useful when the first search strategy does not achieve the desired results online. The searcher must be willing and able to modify the search strategy and keep trying, as long as fruitful results seem likely.

Exhibit 4.1. Sample Lists of Synonyms or Alternative Terms for Concepts

1. vitamin C
   ascorbic acid
2. colleges
   universities
   higher education
   post secondary education
3. police
   law enforcement
   criminal justice
4. senior citizens
   older adults
   elderly
   aged
   aging
5. transportation
   mass transit
   automobiles
   buses
   trains
6. aluminum
   aluminium (British spelling)
7. cities
   urban areas
8. exceptional children
   gifted children
   talented children
9. Great Lakes
   Lake Erie
   Lake Huron
   Lake Superior
   Lake Michigan
   Lake Ontario

EXERCISES

Five search questions which represent a range of subject areas are presented. In order to provide continuity of instruction, these search questions will form the basis for the exercises for Chapters 4, 5, 6, and 7. In this chapter, you are asked to formulate search strategies for each question. In subsequent chapters, you will be asked to perform searches and select appropriate databases and vocabulary terms.

Assume that a client has the following information needs. Formulate a simple search strategy for each. It is not necessary to extract the correct terms from a controlled vocabulary for these exercises.

1. Locate information on issues associated with nuclear reactor safety. The client is not a technical expert and wants articles from the popular literature.
2. Find articles which discuss strategic planning or long-range planning in the automotive industry.
3. Locate information on women in higher education (as administrators, teachers, or students).
4. Are there any references available on the use of computer-assisted instruction or personal computers in the high school classroom?
5. Identify articles on the use of art therapy or music therapy with patients who are schizophrenic or autistic. Do not include any articles which discuss patients with depression.

5

Conducting the Online Search

One of the aims of this text is to support experiential learning in online searching. Although it is only through actual interaction with an information retrieval system that the dynamic nature of online searching is fully appreciated, the basic steps of the search process can be summarized here. This chapter reviews each step, with examples, in order to acquaint the reader with the dynamics of online searching.

The discussion will be limited to the three major commercial information retrieval systems that offer access to multiple databases: DIALOG, SDC ORBIT, and BRS. These three systems are the most universally available and offer the widest variety of services among the commercial systems.

This chapter is intended to be used in conjunction with the reference manuals provided by one or more of the three systems. If the reader has access to one of these systems, the sample searches should be replicated. The system reference manuals will identify any system-specific information required. Exercises for online practice are included at the end of the chapter.

STEPS IN CONDUCTING A SEARCH

Once the information needs of the client are defined, the searcher then holds a reference interview to determine the substance and scope of the search. The search strategy can be organized in a crude form, independent of any specific requirements which will be imposed by the database or search system.

The next step is the selection of appropriate databases to search, depending on the subject content of the request. A precise search strategy is prepared, taking into consideration the unique characteristics of the database(s) to be searched.

In order to execute the strategy, the searcher must first connect the terminal to the appropriate computer. The connection is made using a telephone and a telecommunications network (also referred to as a "value-added network"). This process is known as "logging on" or "signing on."

Once connected to the computer, the searcher requests access to the specific database to be searched and performs the search, modifying the strategy as necessary based on the results. When the strategy is perfected, references are printed online or ordered from the search service vendor (also known as "offline printing"). When the search is completed, the searcher disconnects the terminal from the system -- a procedure known as "logging off" or "signing off." If there are problems with the search, it may be necessary to "log off" and reformulate the search strategy before trying it again.

To review, the process of conducting an online search normally consists of the following steps:

1. Written information request
2. Reference interview
3. Selecting appropriate database(s)
4. Formulating the search strategy
5. Logging on
6. Executing the search
7. Printing relevant items
8. Logging off

The first four steps in the process are addressed in other chapters of this text. This chapter addresses the basic techniques required to complete the actual *online* search activity.

LOGGING ON

The basic steps involved in connecting to a search system computer are the same for each of the three major systems. Exact procedures for making the connection (logging on) are described in the reference manuals.

The first step in logging on is to make the telecommunications connection, usually through one of the two major telecommunications networks, TELENET and TYMNET. Be sure that the terminal is plugged in and turned on; this is often forgotten by beginning searchers.

Find the telephone number for the local node on the telecommunications network. (It can be located in the system reference manual or in documentation from the network.) Make the telephone call to the local network node. The call will be answered with a high-pitched tone; no human voice will be heard. The phone receiver should be placed in the acoustic coupler, if one is used, with the cord in the proper position. The word "cord" usually is apparent on the coupler to indicate the proper direction in which the receiver should be placed. If a dataset or modem is used in place of a coupler, the proper switches should be set.

On most terminals, a light will be illuminated when a connection to the telecommunications network has been made. The light indicates that the terminal is now "online." At this point, the searcher must provide the network with the code name of the search system desired. (Any special code names required, such as those for a specific search system computer or type of terminal, can be found in the system's reference manuals or in documentation supplied by the telecommunications network.) The network will connect the terminal to the requested computer. Once this connection has been achieved, the searcher must provide one or more passwords to indicate that he or she is an authorized user of that system. For security reasons, passwords are not shown on the terminal display, though they are transmitted to the computer. The passwords also ensure that the charges for the search session will be billed properly and that any records ordered for offline printing will be mailed to the correct address.

Passwords are obtained from the search system vendors as part of the original contractual arrangements for system access. The contract binds the holder to pay any charges incurred while the password is in use. Therefore, passwords should be guarded closely.

When the logon procedure is completed, the system will offer the searcher the opportunity to view pertinent news items or messages related to the system. In some cases, this information is automatically printed on the terminal; in others the user is given the option to see the "news" or skip directly to conducting the search. This is the last step in the logon process; the searcher is now ready to select a database and execute the search strategy.

(When green light on terminal appears, user hits carriage return twice *[2 cr]***)**

(Note: User input is shown in italics in these examples.)

```
TELENET
412 6J
```

(Added notes are shown in this typeface.)

TERMINAL= *[1 cr]*

@c 315 20BR **("Address" of search system requested)**

```
315 20B CONNECTED

ENTER BRS PASSWORD
MMMMMM-I-S PASSWORD
MMMMMMM
03 MESSAGES PENDING IN MSGS
```

(User enters password assigned by search system.)

```
ACCESS VIA TELENET

BROADCAST MESSAGE CHANGED 05/24/83 AT 14:58:37.
```

ENTER 'Y' or 'N' for BROADCAST MESSAGE._: *y*

```
THE ONTARIO EDUCATION RESOURCES INFORMATION DATABASE IS NOW AVAILABLE
   (ONED). SEE NEWS DOC 21 FOR DETAILS. REGISTER NOW FOR BRS UPDATES
   DURING MLA,SLA, AND ALA, AND OTHER LOCATIONS IN JUNE. SEE NEWS DOCS 8
   AND 10 FOR DETAILS.
   MDOC IS NO LONGER AVAILABLE. SUPERINDEX FREE TIME-SEE NEWS DOC 22.
   CONTINUE TO USE THE OLD GUIDE FOR BIOL & THE NEW AID PAGE FOR BIOB.
```

ENTER DATA BASE NAME_: *eric* **(No default database; user must select database desired)**

+SIGN-ON 13.41.37 **(Time of day)** 05/25/83: **(Date)**

BRS/ERIC/1966 - MAY 1983 (BOTH)

BRS - SEARCH MODE - ENTER QUERY **(Log-on process is complete; system is now ready to receive search strategy.)**

1-: **(BRS user cue)**

Figure 5.1 Logon to BRS via TELENET.

Figures 5.1 and 5.2 are samples of the logon procedures for the BRS/Search system. Logon procedures to BRS through TELENET are shown in Figure 5.1; procedures for TYMNET are shown in Figure 5.2. Note the minor differences between them. Procedures for DIALOG and SDC are very similar and can be seen in subsequent examples of searches on those systems. Since the systems change from time to time, all specific system or network protocols shown in the text should be verified against appropriate documentation before using them.

```
PLEASE TYPE YOUR TERMINAL IDENTIFIER        (User must enter an
-2435:01-023-                                identifier for the type of
                                             terminal.  No carriage return
                                             used here.)
PLEASE LOG IN: brs (Name of search system)
+ [1 cr]
  REMOTE:  CALL CONNECTED

ENTER BRS PASSWORD
MMMMMMMMM                                    (User enters password)
ENTER A-M-I-S PASSWORD
MMMMMMMMM

03 MESSAGES PENDING IN MSGS

ACCESS VIA TYMNET

BROADCAST MESSAGE CHANGED 05/24/83 AT 14:58:37.
ENTER 'Y' OR 'N' FOR BROADCAST MESSAGE._:  y

THE ONTARIO EDUCATION RESOURCES INFORMATION DATABASE IS NOW AVAILABLE
  (ONED). SEE NEWS DOC 21 FOR DETAILS. REGISTER NOW FOR BRS UPDATES
  DURING MLA,SLA, AND ALA, AND OTHER LOCATIONS IN JUNE. SEE NEWS DOCS 8
  AND 10 FOR DETAILS.
  MDOC IS NO LONGER AVAILABLE. SUPERINDEX FREE TIME-SEE NEWS DOC 22.
  CONTINUE TO USE THE OLD GUIDE FOR BIOL & THE NEW AID PAGE FOR BIOB.

ENTER DATA BASE NAME_:    mesh

+SIGN-ON   13.44.07                05/25/83:

BRS/MESH/1979 - JUN 1983

BRS - SEARCH MODE  - ENTER QUERY
    1_:
```

Figure 5.2 Logon to BRS via TYMNET.

EXECUTING THE SEARCH

Once the terminal has been connected to the search system, the next step is to select a database or file to be searched. Large databases may be divided into several different sections or "files," based on date or some other criteria. The files are stored as though they were separate databases, and each must be searched individually. The terms "database" and "file" are used interchangeably by some authors; this text uses "database" to refer to a computer-searchable set of records unless a "file" that is only part of a database is specifically intended.

In some systems, such as DIALOG, the searcher is connected automatically to a "default" database or file upon logging on. (The default database is usually selected by the searcher as part of the contract; the system supplies the default database associated with the password.) In order to search a different database, a command must be given to tell the computer to change databases. In other systems, such as BRS, the user is not automatically connected to any database but is prompted by the system to select one.

Each system has a "user cue" or "prompt symbol" which indicates that a response from the searcher is expected. The three systems under discussion have these prompt symbols:

System	*Prompt*
DIALOG	?
SDC	SS#/
BRS	_:

These prompts are apparent in the sample searches. Each system also has a list of acceptable commands or "protocol" for operating the system. (The complete set of commands is known as a system's *protocol.*) The searcher must explicitly command the system to take an action, such as select a database or print records online. The commands for each system are listed in their respective system manuals. The commands are annotated in the sample searches. It is important to note that the same word may be used as a command in two different systems, with a different meaning for each. Therefore, it is imperative that the searcher become familiar with the commands for each system to be used.

```
ENTER YOUR DIALOG PASSWORD
MMMMMMMM  LOGON FILE1 WED 25MAY83 12:44:47 PORT058

++ FILE 17 IS UNAVAILABLE ON TELENET
++     FILE 36 IS NOT WORKING
?news news:
   +NEW IMPROVED TYMNET NOW AVAILABLE+
  FREE TIME OFFER IN MAY:
    ENVIRONMENTAL BIBLIOGRAPHY (#68)
  NOW AVAILABLE:
    UPI NEWS (FILE 261)
    CHEMICAL EXPOSURE (FILE 138)
  ANNOUNCEMENTS:
    PRICE CHANGE FOR COFFEELINE (#164)
? begin eric                                (BEGIN command is
          25MAY83 12:45:11 USER2549          used to select database
    $0.20  0.008 HRS FILE1+                  desired.)
    $0.06  TYMNET
    $0.26  ESTIMATED TOTAL COST


FILE1+:ERIC - 66-83/APR
        SET ITEMS DESCRIPTION
        --- ----- -----------
*?  select mainstreaming                    (SELECT command may be used on
                                             DIALOG when requesting postings)
           1  3026 MAINSTREAMING  (PROGRESSIVELY INCLUDING AND MAINTA
*?  select mental retardation
           2  7095 MENTAL RETARDATION  (INTELLECTUAL FUNCTIONING THAT
*?  select elementary education
           3 26385 ELEMENTARY EDUCATION  (EDUCATION PROVIDED IN KINDE
*?  select s1 and s2 and S3
           4    35  S1 AND S2 AND S3  (SELECT command may also
```

Figure 5.3 ERIC database search on the DIALOG system.

```
? type 4/6/1-3
4/6/1
EJ266788
MAINSTREAMING: PARENTAL PERCEPTIONS.
```

be used on DIALOG when introducing Boolean operators with previously retrieved search statements. An alternative method involves the use of the COMBINE command.)

*(These four statements are the long form of entering the search strategy)

```
4/6/2
EJ260705
 A  PARADIGM  FOR PHYSICAL EDUCATION FOR HANDICAPPED CHILDREN IN THE LEAST
RESTRICTIVE ENVIRONMENT.

4/6/3
EJ250292
  MAINSTREAMING AND THE CONSERVANCY.

? ss mainstreaming and mental retardation and elementary education
            5  3026 MAINSTREAMING  (PROGRESSIVELY INCLUDING AND MAINTA
            6  7095 MENTAL RETARDATION  (INTELLECTUAL FUNCTIONING THAT
            7 26385 ELEMENTARY EDUCATION  (EDUCATION PROVIDED IN KINDE
            8    35  5 AND 6 AND 7
?  logoff

          25MAY83 12:48:17 USER2549
   $1.33  0.053 HRS FILE1+ 6 DESCRIPTORS
   $0.42  TYMNET
   $1.75  ESTIMATED TOTAL COST
```

(DIALOG allows for short-cut in entering all terms at once. SS=Abbreviation for SELECT. Note that the use of Boolean operators here allows for both selection and combining of terms at the same time. Set 8 shows the 35 postings which result.)

Figure 5.3 (continued)

```
ENTER BRS PASSWORD
MMMMMMMM-I-S PASSWORD
MMMMMMMM
03 MESSAGES PENDING IN MSGS

ACCESS VIA TELENET

BROADCAST MESSAGE CHANGED 05/24/83 AT 14:58:37.
ENTER 'Y' OR 'N' FOR BROADCAST MESSAGE._:      n
ENTER DATA BASE NAME_:    eric              (Database of choice
                                             is requested.)

+SIGN-ON   13.51.30         05/28/83:

BRS/ERIC/1966 - MAY 1983  (BOTH)
                                            (No command needed for searching
BRS - SEARCH MODE  - ENTER QUERY             of terms on BRS. Terms are
                                             simply entered in search mode.)
    1_:   mainstreaming and gifted or mental-retardation
    RESULT     7208

    2_:   mainstreaming and gifted or mainstreaming and mental-retardation
    RESULT      337

    3_:   mainstreaming                     (Note that compound
    RESULT     3072                          terms are hyphenated.)

    4_:   gifted or mental-retardation
    RESULT    10982                         (Note: High retrieval
                                             of postings in Search
    5_:   3 and 4                            Statement 1 due to
```

Figure 5.4 ERIC on BRS.

```
RESULT      337
```

retrieval of all items on mental retardation. Also, Search Statement 2 is short-cut version of Search Statements 3 through 5.)

```
6_:  ..print 5 ti/doc=1-3
```

(PRINT Command to check titles for relevance.)

```
     1
TI INDIVIDUALIZED INSTRUCTION: IMPLICATIONS FOR THE GIFTED.

     2
TI PROVIDING FOR THE MATHEMATICALLY GIFTED CHILD IN THE REGULAR
   ELEMENTARY CLASSROOM.

     3
TI THE GIFTED CHILD IN THE ORDINARY CLASSROOM.

               END OF DOCUMENTS

_:     ..off
```

(Logoff command)

```
+CONNECT TIME   0:02:19 HH:MM:SS  0.039 DEC HRS   SESSION 1339+

EST ERIC COST:  C-HRS  DB-ROY  CIT-ROY  COMM  TOTAL
                 $.62   $.00     $.00    $.27  $.89
+SIGN-OFF  13.53.22      05/25/83:

15 20B DISCONNECTED
```

(Estimated charges)

Figure 5.4 (continued)

The search is now conducted using the search strategy which was developed before logging on. The sample search shown in Figure 5.3 is the result of a request for references on the topic, "mainstreaming of retarded children in elementary schools." The ERIC database was selected as the most appropriate to the topic; since it uses a controlled vocabulary, the thesaurus was examined. These ERIC subject headings were selected: "mainstreaming," "mental retardation" (used for "retarded children"), and "elementary education." The terms are connected with an AND, resulting in the following search strategy:

mainstreaming AND mental retardation AND elementary education

The search strategy may be entered in one string, as shown above, or the terms may be entered individually and then combined using the Boolean AND. The end result is the same – only records containing all three terms will be retrieved. Figure 5.3 illustrates the sample search performed on the ERIC database using the DIALOG system. Both methods of entering the search strategy are illustrated.

Most inexperienced searchers find it less confusing to use separate statements for each term or concept because the way the system will handle the terms is made more explicit. Each system has a precedence (priority) order for processing the Boolean operators. In most retrieval systems (and in all three under discussion), the AND and AND NOT operators will be processed before the OR operator. If only one operator is used, the search statement is unambiguous. If different operators are used, the statement can be ambiguous and should be clarified either by entering the search statements separately and combining them as intended or by using parentheses to clarify the order of processing.

For example, if the search request were for documents on "mainstreaming of gifted OR retarded children," the search strategy would require clarification. If converted into the strategy, "mainstreaming AND gifted OR mental retardation," records on "mainstreaming AND gifted children" and records on "mental retardation" would be retrieved. The search is illustrated in Figure 5.4; note that the strategy retrieved 6,730 items because it pulled all records which contained the term "mental retardation."

The intended result of this search request can be achieved in several ways, two of which are illustrated in Figure 5.4:
1) Restate the strategy as "mainstreaming AND gifted OR mainstreaming AND mental retardation;" or 2) enter "mainstreaming"

alone, enter "gifted OR mental retardation" as a separate statement, then combine the two statements with an AND. Another approach would be to enter the strategy as one statement with parentheses: "mainstreaming AND (gifted OR mental retardation)."

Entering search terms individually makes it easier to determine the contribution of each term to the total retrieval, and one can judge whether each concept is too broad or too narrow. Search strategy revision can also be made more easily than if the entire strategy is entered at once.

PRINTING RELEVANT ITEMS

When a sufficient number of items has been retrieved, titles from a few of the retrieved records should be printed online to assess relevance. If the titles are satisfactory, the full records can be printed online or a command given to print them offline and mail them.

Each search system vendor maintains print options for its databases. The term "print options" refers to standardized formats for printing records, varying the portion of the record displayed and in the arrangement. For example, a searcher may request that only titles or only authors and titles be printed. The use of print options can save the connect time cost of printing the full record, while providing enough information to make a cursory judgement of relevance. The full record is normally printed offline. Occasionally it may be necessary to review the full record online in order to check the index terms assigned to the record or to read the abstract.

If the documents retrieved do not appear to be relevant, or if too many irrelevant items are included, the search strategy can be revised. Simple revision is a principal advantage of interactive searching. More specific terms may be selected or broad terms deleted. Reviewing index terms in relevant documents may suggest appropriate terms for use in the strategy.

The refining process can continue indefinitely. Few search strategies are ever perfect. If there are major problems with the retrieval, it may be more cost-effective to logoff and reconsider the strategy before trying again.

Figures 5.5, 5.6, and 5.7 illustrate completed searches on each of the three systems. The reader should compare the searches and note differences in the command languages and formats

```
c 415 48

415 48 CONNECTED

ENTER YOUR DIALOG PASSWORD
MMMMMMMMM  LOGON FILE1 WED 25MAY83 12:53:49 Port070


++ FILE 17 IS UNAVAILABLE ON TELENET
++     FILE 36 IS NOT WORKING
? news news:
   +NEW IMPROVED TYMNET NOW AVAILABLE+
  FREE TIME OFFER IN MAY:
    ENVIRONMENTAL BIBLIOGRAPHY (#68)
  NOW AVAILABLE:
    UPI NEWS (FILE 261)
    CHEMICAL EXPOSURE (FILE 138)
  ANNOUNCEMENTS:
    PRICE CHANGE FOR COFFEELINE (#164)
? begin eric
       25MAY83 12:54:12 USER2549
    $0.20  0.008 HRS FILE1+
    $0.06  TELENET
    $0.26  ESTIMATED TOTAL COST


FILE1+:ERIC - 66-83/APR
         SET ITEMS DESCRIPTION
         --- ----- -----------

? s mainstreaming; s mental retardation; s elementary education
           1  3026 MAINSTREAMING  (PROGRESSIVELY INCLUDING AND MAINTA
           2  7095 MENTAL RETARDATION  (INTELLECTUAL FUNCTIONING THAT
           3 26385 ELEMENTARY EDUCATION  (EDUCATION PROVIDED IN KINDE
? c 1and2and3
           4    35 1AND2AND3
? ss s1 and s2 and s3

           5    35 1 AND 2 AND 3
? print4/5/1-35
PRINTED4/5/1-35 ESTIMATED COST: $3.50 (TO CANCEL, ENTER PR-)
? pr-
CANCELLED PRINT 4/5/1-35
? logoff
           25MAY83 12:55:50 USER2549
    $0.73  0.029 HRS FILE1+ 3 DESCRIPTORS
    $0.23  TELENET
    $0.96  ESTIMATED TOTAL COST

LOGOFF 12:55:58

415 48 DISCONNECTED
```

(DIALOG allows for "stacking" of commands. Simply separate by semi-colon as done here.)

(Note Offline Print Command and Print Format Requested. Online Print Command is TYPE)

(Approximated time and cost data given.)

Figure 5.5 DIALOG search.

```
c 315 20br

315 20B CONNECTED

ENTER BRS PASSWORD
MMMMMMMMM-I-S PASSWORD
MMMMMMMMMM
03 MESSAGES PENDING IN MSGS

ACCESS VIA TELENET

BROADCAST MESSAGE CHANGED 05/24/83 AT 14:58:37.
ENTER 'Y' OR 'N' FOR BROADCAST MESSAGE._:   n
ENTER DATA BASE NAME_:    eric
+SIGN-ON   13.58.06                5/25/83:

BRS/ERIC/1966 - MAY 1983 (BOTH)

BRS - SEARCH MODE  - ENTER QUERY
    1_:    mainstreaming
    RESULT    3072

    2_:    mental-retardation
    RESULT    7115

    3_:    elementary-education
   RESULT   26558

    4_:    1 and 2 and 3
    RESULT      35

    5_:     ..printoff 4 bibl/doc=all/id=patti corbett
YOUR OFFLINE QUERY HAS BEEN SAVED UNDER THE NAME OF Q0549
                (Note: Commands in BRS are preceded by ".."
                 Items will now be printed offline and mailed.)

_:     ..off
+CONNECT TIME   0:01:59 HH:MM:SS   0.033 DEC HRS   SESSION 1340+

EST ERIC COST   C-HRS   DB-ROY   CIT-ROY  COMM  TOTAL

                $.53    $.00     $.00     $.23  $.76

+SIGN-OFF  13.59.24                5/25/83:
315 20B DISCONNECTED                  (Note approximate cost
                                       data and sign-off time.)
```

(Note: Search could also be entered in one step using "command stacking." Terms to be searched could be entered in a series on one line separated by a slash [/].)

Figure 5.6 Sample BRS search.

```
PROG:
++++
FEDREG, CRECORD NOW HAVE SDI SERVICE: SEE NEWS.
++++
YOU ARE NOW CONNECTED TO THE ORBIT DATABASE.
FOR A TUTORIAL, ENTER A QUESTION MARK.  OTHERWISE, ENTER A COMMAND.


USER:
file eric

PROG:
ELAPSED TIME ON ORBIT: 0.01 HRS.
YOU ARE NOW CONNECTED TO THE ERIC DATABASE.
COVERS RIE 1966 THRU MAR (8303) AND CIJE 1969 THRU MAR (8303)

SS 1 /0?
USER:
mainstreaming                  (Stacking can also be used quite easily
                                on SDC, i.e. mainstreaming; mental
PROG:                           retardation; elementary education;
SS 1 PSTG (3001)                1 and 2 and 3)

SS 2 /0?
USER:
mental retardation

PROG:
SS 2 PSTG (7081)

SS 3 /0?
USER:
elementary education

PROG:
SS 3 PSTG (26191)

SS 4 /0?
USER:
1 and 2 and 3

PROG:
SS 4 PSTG (35)

SS 5 /0?
USER:
print 3 ti
```

Figure 5.7 Sample SDC search.

for searching. Each search ends with a "logoff" command; if additional databases were to be searched, a database request command would be given instead.

SUMMARY

The process of searching consists of a series of steps, beginning with the written information request and ending with logging off the system. This chapter covered the steps after the information had been gathered and the search strategy defined.

The actual online search begins by connecting the local terminal to a search system through a telecommunications connection. Once connected and logged on, a database is selected and the search statements are entered. The exact commands used vary by system.

Search strategies can be entered in steps or all in one statement. Entering a search strategy in individual steps has the advantage of determining the contribution of each part of the statement, although it takes longer. When entering a search strategy with several Boolean operators, it is important to clarify any ambiguities in the order of execution, either through the use of parentheses or by breaking it into several statements.

Once a sufficient number of matches has been retrieved, a few should be displayed online to determine relevance. If satisfactory, they can be printed offline and mailed. Printing is usually the last step of a search, although the whole process from selecting a database through printing can be repeated indefinitely in an online search.

Examples of simple searches on each of the three major commercial systems, DIALOG, SDC, and BRS, were provided. The searches can be replicated in these systems, but the commands should be verified against system manuals for accuracy, as changes do occur.

Only the most basic commands and capabilities have been presented. The next two chapters provide important background for more advanced searching, and specific skills will be developed further in Chapter 8.

EXERCISES

The following are information requests from a client. Perform the search for each question, using one or more of the databases suggested. Use the search strategy which was developed in the exercises for Chapter 4, modifying as needed for the database selected. The searches may be performed on any of the three search systems, DIALOG, SDC ORBIT, or BRS.

The suggested databases may have different names in each search system. The names given here are those of the printed indexes, as names vary between search systems. The search system database directory will provide the exact database name, which will be similar to the index name, or indicate that the printed index is the source of the database material. Not all of these databases are available on each search system.

1. Locate information on issues associated with nuclear reactor safety. The client is a technical expert and wants articles from the scientific literature.
   Databases: Compendex, Physics Abstracts, Engineering Index, NTIS
2. Find articles which discuss strategic planning or long-range planning in the automotive industry.
   Databases: ABI Inform, Management Contents, Predicasts
3. Locate information on women in higher education (as administrators, teachers, or students).
   Database: ERIC
4. Are there any references available on the use of computer-assisted instruction or personal computers in the high school classroom?
   Databases: ERIC, Social Science Citation Index, Magazine Index
5. Identify articles on the use of art therapy or music therapy with patients who are schizophrenic or autistic. Do not include any articles which discuss patients with depression.
   Database: Psychological Abstracts

6

Databases

A thorough knowledge of the structure and content of a database is basic to the training of a search analyst. Yet, it would be impossible to do justice to the topic as a whole without placing stringent limits on the scope of the discussion. Thus, the following points are covered only to the extent that they affect the ability of the search intermediary to conduct an online bibliographic search: the origin of databases and the structure of the industry; types of databases and their relationship with printed indexes; selecting the appropriate databases; the internal makeup and structure of a typical database, including elements of standardization; the relationship between databases and information retrieval systems; and finally, where to turn for more information on a given database.

As mentioned in Chapter 1, a database refers to any organized collection of related computer-readable data. In this particular case, emphasis is entirely upon those databases which are searchable through the large, multi-database, commercial information retrieval systems. However, one should not lose sight of the fact that information contained in many such databases has previously been available in a printed format, namely the index. A collection of databases, such as those offered by a search system vendor, is sometimes referred to as a "databank."

In a library context, most electronic databases are based on an equivalent printed index but offer greater flexibility and sophistication in the searching process. Computer capabilities can be utilized to take advantage of multiple access points to each entry, and logical relationships can be required among entries to refine a query further.

ORIGIN OF DATABASES

Although the capability of producing electronic databases coincided with the production of the first computer, the practicality of the venture depended upon the ability to search large volumes of data at a low cost per search. Therefore, not only was it necessary to wait for appropriate electronic storage facilities, but it was also essential to consider the cost of the original input.

As computer technology became more sophisticated, it gradually infiltrated every labor-intensive industry. One such area was the printing and publishing business. The advent of photocomposition (electronic typesetting) revolutionized the printing process and created a marketable by-product: the computerized form of a printed index.

Continued technological advances, a growing confidence in computers, and an urgent need to process quickly the ever-increasing volume of data to be published, led to the production of the first commercially-available databases in the mid-1960's. It would be another five years before the time-sharing generation of computers and the lowered cost and larger capacities of online storage would make the online database practical as a medium for information storage and transfer.

STRUCTURE OF THE DATABASE INDUSTRY

The structure of the database industry runs parallel to that of the book publishing industry, with the added complications that the electronic product can be disseminated in a variety of forms and there is a high degree of overlap among the various segments of the industry. The picture which was once so sharp in the traditional publishing trade is much less clear in the area of electronic publishing.

In other words, there still are the producers, the vendors, the libraries and information centers, and the information seekers. And as is the case in traditional publishing, individuals or organizations can and do cross the lines to bypass certain segments and combine others to shorten the distance between the producer of an idea and its ultimate user.

However, keep in mind that the printed equivalent of the database is actually a hard copy "index" or a collection of references, as opposed to a single book. A database can be the equivalent of a reference collection in computer-readable form, and as such it can be very costly to own and maintain. The high cost of individual ownership, operation, and maintenance of multiple databases has given rise to the existence of the commercial information retrieval systems.

To follow this through with a single database in mind, the process is begun by an organization generating the magnetic tape containing the appropriate records in computer-readable form. This organization may or may not offer its own search system, but in all likelihood is willing to sell or lease the tape to a commercial search system vendor. The vendor, in turn, must manipulate the data on the tape to fit its own software requirements. Indexes must be created, and new tapes must be merged periodically with older editions of the same database to update the files. At this point the vendor is ready to share the contents of the database with a library or information center for a fixed service fee and/or hourly rates applicable to that database, or it may opt to sell the service directly to the end user or client employing its own staff of search intermediaries.

Examples of some database producers who do not provide supporting computer software for search purposes include the Chemical Abstracts Service (CAS) and Engineering Index (EI). The INSPEC database (from the Institution of Electrical Engineers) falls into the category of those databases whose producer provides only a partial search service; in this case the service is limited to selective dissemination of information (SDI) searches. None of the above producers provides the full text of the documents referenced in their databases.

The National Technical Information Service (NTIS) of the U.S. Department of Commerce is a database producer which has the responsibility for disseminating the scientific, engineering, and technical documents produced under federally-funded projects. As such, it falls into a category of centers offering a much wider range of services. Its database can be accessed by individuals through the NTIS search service. It is available through several commercial vendors as well. Full text of the documents are available from this database producer. The National Library of Medicine's MEDLINE is an example of a system which both produces the database and provides the software for retrieving medical information.

And finally, The Information Bank (of The New York Times) is a good example of a database producer who goes full circle between the originator of the document and its user. Not only is every permutation of the chain of usage covered, but the original contents of the database can be accessed readily by those who helped produce those very documents: the reporters and editorial staff of The New York Times. The New York Times recently relinquished marketing control of the system, licensing the search service to Mead Data Central for exclusive distribution.

TYPES OF DATABASES

Reviewing the definition of a database as an organized collection of related computer-readable data, and then looking at the proliferation of automated systems, it becomes apparent that whereever there is a problem of storing large quantities of information, a potential database exists. From banks and supermarkets, to the space program and international cooperative efforts in every field, records are being organized and stored in computerized form. Thus, it would be futile to attempt an exhaustive listing of all types of databases available.

Limiting discussion to those databases available through commercial retrieval systems, however, the files can be categorized in two ways. One option is to divide all databases into either *bibliographic* or *nonbibliographic* – bibliographic are those containing references to literature, and nonbibliographic are those containing source data, which may be either numerical or representational in form.

Although the majority of databases in existence today are of the nonbibliographic variety, these files are more likely to be accessed directly by the end users, leaving the bibliographic databases as the major domain of the search intermediary. Thus, a second option for categorizing databases, which may be more valid in the context of this chapter, would be to identify them on the basis of whether they are "reference" or "source."

Reference Databases

Reference databases are compilations of records that refer the user to a source document but which do not in themselves contain the full text of the source document. The majority of commercially-available databases used in a library setting fall into this category. Each "unit record" within such a database may contain a simple citation (author, title, and source) alone or in combination with one or more of the following elements: controlled index terms, uncontrolled index terms, abstracts, and other appropriate category or index codes. The Agriculture On-Line Access (AGRICOLA) database of the U.S. Department of Agriculture is a typical reference database which contains references to journal articles, government reports, and monographs, providing worldwide coverage in the field of agriculture and related areas. The AGRICOLA record contains a citation supplemented by an abstract and by controlled index terms covering the subject areas of food, nutrition, and agricultural economics.

The *citation database* is a variant of the bibliographic database. It provides a citation map of the literature as well as reference to the documents which do the citing. Science Citation Index and Social Science Citation Index are examples of bibliographic citation indexes.

Source Databases

Although there is much greater variety in the types of databases that can be called source databases, they still form a minor portion of the total files available through the three major online retrieval systems. Numeric, textual-numeric, properties, and full-text databases exemplify the type of database which can yield immediate and complete results in a single search because it contains the full amount of information being sought by the end user.

Numeric databases may include credit or banking information, statistical documents such as those of the U.S. Bureau of the Census, or economic data such as the Dow Jones News Retrieval Service. Statistical abstracts and tables offered by PROMT (Predicasts Overview of Markets and Technology), which contains Census Bureau data, may be sufficient to answer many basic queries, although the full text of the document is not available online.

Dictionary databases are comprised of nonbibliographic records which pertain to a special subject area or field. Chemical compounds, classification codes, and vocabulary databases fall into this category. BIOCODES, produced by the Biosciences Information Service of Biological Abstracts, is a dictionary of Taxonomic-Codes used in BIOSIS databases. This source database contains codes, the broader term/narrower term (also called "genus/species") relationships represented by such codes, and cross-reference terms for every Taxonomic-Code record.

A unit record from CHEMDEX (Chemical Abstracts Service), reproduced from an SDC search, is shown in Figure 6.1. Each record contains the registry number, molecular formula, chemical name, synonyms, and ring system information.

Directory databases such as GRANTS (The Oryx Press), SSIE (Smithsonian Science Information Exchange), USCA (U.S. Contract Awards), and FEDREG (Federal Register), also contain nonbibliographic records which can produce lists of organizations, contracts, hearings, and the like. Although it can be argued that this type of database is primarily "reference," it is included in the "source" category because in many instances the database itself can provide the final answer to a user's query. For example, a record from FEDREG can identify rules, proposed rules, public law notices, meetings, hearings, and presidential proclamations on a variety of topics including athletics, business, consumer affairs, environment, taxation, transportation, and veterans' affairs. The substance of a rule or the date of a hearing may be the only information required by the client. In such instances, this database becomes the final source for the information at hand.

```
RN  - 69-52-3
MF  - C16H19N3O4S.Na
N   - 4-Thia-1-azabicyclo(3.2.0)heptane-2-carboxylic acid,
      6-((aminophenylacetyl)amino)-3,3-dimethyl-7-oxo-, monosodium salt,
      (2S-(2.alpha.,5.alpha.,6.beta.(S*)))-
RSD - 1 ring, C6
RSD - 2 rings, C3N,C3NS (NCSC2)
SYNM- 4-Thia-1-azabicyclo(3.2.0)heptane-2-carboxylic acid,
      6-(2-amino-2-phenylacetamido)-3,3-dimethyl-7-oxo-, monosodium salt,
      D-(-)- (Also 8CI); Ampicillin sodium; Penbritin-S; Sodium P-50;
      Sodium 6-(D-.alpha.-aminophenylacetamido)penicillanoate; Sodium
      ampicillin; Ampicillin sodium salt; Binotal sodium; Sodium
      D-.alpha.-aminobenzylpenicillanate; Sodium binotal;
      D-.alpha.-Aminobenzylpenicillin sodium salt; Polycillin N
```

Figure 6.1

Legal databases which contain the full text of legal codes or court decisions meet all of the criteria of a source database also. For example, WESTLAW and LEXIS provide the capability for full-text searching of the U.S. Code, Supreme Court decisions, and many other source documents from federal, state, and local courts and governments.

Generally, a full-text database refers to a file which contains an entire document. However, as is evident from the above list of source databases, any file which contains the complete text of the information being sought – whether a formula, a definition, a date, or a statistic – is by definition a full-text database.

In the actual work environment, categorizing client queries is likely to be just as important as categorizing databases. What is important is to deduce the needs of the client and to decide whether the abstract of a record contains sufficient information to satisfy those needs. Ultimately, it is this analysis which determines whether a database is in fact the "source" or merely a "reference" to the source of information required by a given individual.

ONLINE VS. PRINTED INDEXES

In looking carefully at the databases mentioned above, numerous files can be found whose history dates back to the days of printed indexes. In fact, many are still published in hard copy form in addition to being available in an electronic medium. Following are a few examples of computerized databases and their printed counterparts.

Computer-Readable Databases	Printed Publications
AGRICOLA	Bibliography of Agriculture
BIOSIS Previews	Biological Abstracts Bioresearch Index
FEDREG	Federal Register Abstracts
GRANTS	Grant Information System Faculty Alert Bulletin
INSPEC	Physics Abstracts Electrical & Electronic Abstracts Computer and Control Abstracts

As mentioned previously, many of these databases were in fact created as by-products of the printed index. However, numerous databases have been developed during the past decade that do not have a printed counterpart. Thus, retrospective searches in these files are as dependent upon the online systems as are current awareness updates. For example, SDC's Forest Products database (Forest Products Research Society) covers the worldwide literature of the entire wood products industry since 1947. There is no printed publication which replicates the same coverage. With source materials ranging from journals and government publications to patents and abstracted bulletins and monographs, the comprehensive nature of this database dictates its use whenever a wood-industry-related search is required.

Most online databases have developed and grown beyond the limits of their printed versions. Many of the limits imposed upon the printed index are space- and time-related:

1. There is a physical limit to the size of a printed volume. Each additional index entry increases the size of the book, making it harder to handle and more difficult to store. The storage problem increases with the addition of every volume produced to accommodate the growing number of entries.
2. There is a time/cost factor in producing a printed volume. Each additional index entry increases the time spent by the indexer to select, authenticate, and apply the new entry to the index.
3. There is a time/cost factor related to the updating of a printed index. Not only is there an inherent time lag in the publishing process, but it is also costly to provide subsequent updates to the index.

These problems are not insurmountable in a manual indexing system, but they are more readily addressed and resolved by the online database and index. However, the following capabilities offered by the computer cannot realistically be replicated manually:

1. *Full-text searching*. References or entire documents may be retrieved by *any* significant term contained within the text. Time and space limitations make this option unacceptably expensive in a manual indexing system.
2. *Logical search capabilities*. It is possible to link many concepts in a manner which would be impractical for the manual searcher.

3. *Sorting and sequencing capabilities*. The computer can automatically generate an output list which meets the specific criteria desired by the searcher. The list can be weighted so that the most relevant or most recent records appear at the top. It can be sorted alphabetically (or chronologically) according to the searcher's instructions. In other words, the output can be customized by the computer without requiring additional human effort.
4. *File maintenance*. The index vocabulary can be updated continuously. Older records can be merged with new ones. Obsolete and erroneous records can be purged from the files.
5. *Selective Dissemination of Information (SDI)*. By placing a one-time standing order, the user automatically obtains updates in a field of special interest. This current awareness service is based on the individual's interest profile and provides the results of a comprehensive literature search on a regular schedule. All three major commercial information retrieval systems offer SDI services on at least a selected portion of their databases.

In light of the above points, it becomes apparent that the flexibility offered by online databases cannot be replicated entirely by the traditional printed index.

SELECTING A DATABASE

Regardless of a searcher's expertise on a given information retrieval system, conducting a successful search is highly dependent on the individual's ability to analyze the query properly and to select the appropriate database(s) for searching.

There are a number of sources which provide basic assistance in choosing the appropriate database for a given search. For example, printed sources such as Hoover's *The Library and Information Manager's Guide to Online Services* and William's *Computer-Readable Data Bases — A Directory and Data Sourcebook* provide excellent overviews of current services and offer a wealth of specific information on numerous bibliographic and nonbibliographic databases.

In addition, each information retrieval system offers a complete description of all databases available through that system. Apart from the many directories, guides, and newsletters available in print or on microform from each vendor, a "database of databases" can also be accessed online. DIALOG's DIALINDEX, SDC's Data Base Index, and BRS/CROS are online sources that can be used to identify all available databases which contain a given term or combination of terms likely to yield positive results for a query. They provide a starting point for a search on an unfamiliar topic and may expand a search beyond the limits of the most obvious databases.

Looking at the approximate number of records that would be retrieved by a given term or search strategy can also provide a good indication of the applicability of a database to a particular query. The number of records per index term is provided online by most databases and retrieval systems; they are also available in list form on microfiche from DIALOG's DIALIST.

When the initial query falls clearly within the limits of a given database, or when the search analyst has access to only a limited number of databases, there is little question as to the choice of databases to be used. However, when there is a need to narrow the field and choose among several available databases, the following questions should be raised to assist the searcher in selecting the most appropriate databases:

- Does the database offer an interdisciplinary approach to a particular topic, or is it geared to the needs of a very specialized user group?
- Is the database related to an existing printed index or indexes, or does it exist only in computer-readable form?
- Are the documents referenced in the database readily available?
- What is its period of literature/data coverage?
- Can it accommodate retrospective searches, and if so, for what period?
- How often is the database updated (how current is the information)?
- Are search aids (including thesauri) readily available?
- How does the cost compare with other sources offering similar information?

Overlap between databases is also a consideration in database selection. Multiple databases in a subject area may incorporate some of the same material. In determining which to search, the above questions should be considered. There may be a difference in focus; one database may be management oriented and another may be technologically oriented, for example. Other considerations might be the type of indexing or the data elements in the unit record – one may have abstracts and the other not.

The type of source document required may determine the choice of databases when subject content is similar. The request may specify (or imply) a particular type of document, such as research-in-progress reports, conference papers, patents, raw data or facts, or journal articles only. The type of material in a database can be determined by reviewing the database documentation supplied by either the database vendor or by the search system vendor.

If a comprehensive search is required, it may be necessary to search databases with a high degree of overlap and recognize that some records will be duplicated. Some systems allow output from searches on different databases to be interfiled before printing, making duplicates easier to identify. For legal reasons of data ownership, it is not possible explicitly to eliminate all duplicates; each database producer wishes to be paid for items retrieved from its database.

In reviewing some of the above questions, the search analyst should bear in mind that the contents of a computer-readable database are basically the same as the printed index counterpart. The type, depth, and scope of literature covered by various databases offered by a retrieval system is not uniform. But if printed counterparts exist, it is wise to spend some time getting acquainted with the subject coverage offline, keeping in mind that updates to the online files are often ahead of the printed indexes.

It is also safe to assume that online files offer a greater volume or variety of index terms. However, such terms may not be wholly transferable across databases. Using a retrieval system's general index terms can overcome some of the basic vocabulary incompatibilities among databases. In most cases, it is necessary to reformat the search strategy to meet the requirements of each database.

THE RELATIONSHIP BETWEEN THE DATABASE AND THE SYSTEM VENDOR

If the database selected is available on more than one search system, the searcher may need to determine on which system it should be accessed. The database producer may lease the same database to multiple vendors, but differences in processing and support will result in differences in the way the database is searched on the various systems. The online vendors expand the searching capabilities of the database in different ways. In processing the database, significant terms may be extracted from a pre-defined set of fields, such as title and abstract. These terms are added to the index files in addition to those controlled vocabulary terms provided by the indexers. Other data may be expanded to make the database more useful, such as converting a language code to a language name. The amount and type of processing, the choice of significant terms extracted, and the fields selected may vary between the systems.

The online vendor processing may limit the searchability of a database in other ways, however. For example, not all of the searchable fields assigned by the database supplier may be retrievable through every search system. The retrospective coverage also may vary from system to system. In some cases the abstracts to individual records in the database may be accessible for full-text searching in one system but not another.

For all of the above reasons, there will be differences in search results when the same database is accessed through different retrieval systems. Most of the differences are due to software capabilities, which are updated or altered frequently, making it difficult to present a precise discussion of specific databases. The reader is referred to Chapter 5 for an example of the same search conducted on multiple systems, and to other literature sources (1).

DATABASE STRUCTURE

Just as a printed book has a physical format which relates to the printed information carried on each page, so does each database have a physical structure which is at once standardized to meet the needs of various retrieval systems and yet customized to serve the requirements of the specific information it must carry. In other words, a student is trained to look for specific types of information in pre-determined locations within the printed format of a book: table of contents in the front, footnotes at the bottom of each page or at the end of each section, and index and glossary at the end. This "standard" fits the majority of non-fiction books on the market today. In the same manner, information retrieval systems are programmed to take advantage of a standard format applied to physical structure of databases.

Every database is made up of a series of *records*. Each record may represent a group of documents (such as a monographic series), a single complete document (such as a court decision, a medical record, or a full text of a document), or a selected portion of a document (such as the journal citation and abstract.

Within each record, the file structure allows for the identification (and tagging) of specific *data elements* (also referred to as *fields* or *subfields*). The initial identification of individual data elements by the database producer is crucial, as it forms the basis for the search structure of the retrieval system. For example, the following elements may be present in, or applicable to, a single document in a bibliographic database:

- Accesssion number or registry code (assigned by the document producer)
- Author(s)
- Title
- Subtitle
- Organizational source (the authors' affiliation or the project's source of support)
- Journal name (or the title of the source document)
- Date
- Language of the full text of the original document
- ISSN/Coden
- Index terms assigned by the database producer
- Supplementary index terms identified by the database producer
- Document type

Any or all such elements, when properly identified by the database producer, can be searched and sorted on by a retrieval system. For example, if a document is written in French and the database producer has allowed for language identification, then the searcher can specify the inclusion or exclusion of that record based on its language. In this case, "language" is regarded as a *searchable field* in the database.

The retrievability of any data element is highly dependent upon the software of the retrieval system. Thus, it is possible to obtain different results by searching the same database on two different retrieval systems. While a primitive search system may be bound closely to the database structure, a sophisticated system can enhance the searchability of poorly designed files. This is especially true of retrieval systems that produce inverted files (i.e., create multiple indexes external to the database). On such systems, any significant term in a database can be searched regardless of the database producer's indexing or field identification procedures.

Despite these alternatives offered by the information retrieval systems, or perhaps because of them, it is essential for the search analyst to become fully acquainted with all searchable fields of the often-used databases, since they can be powerful tools in controlling search results.

For example, when a broad search strategy cannot be contained through vocabulary control and is likely to retrieve too many references, the search can be limited to the "title" field, thereby omitting additional references which may have been retrieved from the "index term" or "abstract" fields. Conversely, when a topic is too new or not likely to be found in the established vocabulary of a field, the analyst may choose to include the searching of uncontrolled index terms from the "abstract" field. Other applications of searching by fields are discussed in Chapter 8.

STANDARDIZATION

As mentioned above, various types of databases require their own unique file structure and data element formatting. With the proliferation of databases during the past decade, and the growth of multi-database search systems, it is becoming apparent that standards are more than a tool of convenience for database producers. Searchers and vendors alike have expressed a strong preference for establishing industry standards as an essential and unifying force in a diverse marketplace. As more pressure is brought to bear on database producers, a gradual trend toward uniformity in the formatting of database tapes and their contents is likely to occur.

An excellent example of a database producer committed to the use of standardized formats is the American Geological Institute's GEOREF Information Services. The following information on the application of national and international standards by GEOREF is provided on page 47 of its *Workshop Training Manual.*

> "Tape format and data element standard: UNISIST Reference Manual for Machine-Readable Bibliographic Descriptions. The data elements in the Standard have been used for GEOREF from October 1975 on . . .
>
> "Word Abbreviation List (Am[erican] Nat[iona]l Standards Inst[titute]) [is] used to abbreviate journal titles, corporate authors, affiliations, meeting names, publishers, etc. Not used for titles, which are not abbreviated.
>
> "Codes for the Representation of Names of Countries, ISO 3166 (Int[ernational] Organ[ization] for Standardization, 1974). The Alpha-3 Code is used for GEOREF."

MULTI-DATABASE SEARCH SYSTEMS

Apart from searching advantages inherent in a given computer-readable database, additional enhancements can be offered by multi-database information retrieval systems carrying that database. The following are among the benefits that accrue from particular retrieval systems:

1. The general index of the search system can be used in conjunction with the database's own specific index, allowing for more comprehensive search strategies. Cross-database searches also become more uniform and flexible, as well as less time-consuming.
2. Multiple database searches can be performed on portions of search strategies (also called "search fragments") stored from previous searches.
3. Capability of free-text searching of at least the citation (author, title, source) fields is offered by the retrieval systems. Added to the use of the database's controlled vocabulary, this option provides for maximum retrieval possibilities. However, when no controlled vocabulary exists, the database is even more dependent on the search capabilities and vocabulary lists of the retrieval system.

4. The search system may add the capability of weighted term searches and other tools such as truncation, adjacency, neighboring, and the like.

SUMMARY

A search analyst is only as successful as the search results produced through the judicious use of available databases. The necessity for familiarization with database content and structure cannot be over-emphasized. Fortunately, a search analyst is not required to be familiar with "all" computerized databases, just as the librarian is not required to be conversant with the entire library's holdings. In fact, many libraries with multiple search analysts frequently assign to each searcher the responsibility for several databases in a given subject area, thus allowing for the development of considerable expertise on specific databases.

It is also important to note that many database vendors offer training in the use of their databases. Workshops and user groups coordinated by these producers permit the search analyst to keep abreast of the latest developments and to share real life problems and solutions with other interested individuals. These and other sources of training are discussed in Chapter 11.

EXERCISES

Assume that the following search requests were asked by a client. Using the database documentation supplied by the database producer and/or the search system vendor, select all the databases which might be appropriate for each query.

Formulate a precise search strategy, customized to the database, for at least two databases for each search request. Compare the strategies constructed for each question on the different databases.

Using the customized search strategy, perform the search on at least one database. Do not search on the same database that you used in the exercises for Chapter 5.

1. Locate information on issues associated with nuclear reactor safety. The client is a technical expert but is preparing a speech for a local consumer group. Information from both the popular and scientific literature is needed.

2. Find articles which discuss strategic planning or long-range planning in the automotive industry.
3. Locate information on women in higher education (as administrators, teachers, or students).
4. Are there any references available on the use of computer-assisted instruction or personal computers in the high school classroom?
5. Identify articles on the use of art therapy or music therapy with patients who are schizophrenic or autistic. Do not include any articles which discuss patients with depression.

FOOTNOTE

1. For comparisons between the three major commercial information retrieval systems, please see the references in the chapter bibliography.

BIBLIOGRAPHY

Bement, James H. "The New Prices – Some Comparisons." *ONLINE*, Vol. 1, No. 2 (1977), p. 9-22.

Blair, John. "Cross-Database Searching a Chemical Compound: Comparing Lockheed, SDC, BRS, and NLM." *ONLINE*, Vol. 5, No. 2 (1981), p. 46-61.

Christian, Roger. *The Electronic Library: Bibliographic Data Bases 1978-79*. White Plains, NY: Knowledge Industry Publications, 1978.

Cuadra, Carlos A. "Bement's Search Times Challenged." (Letter to the editor), *ONLINE*, Vol. 1, No. 4 (1977), p. 3, 90.

Folke, Carolyn. "Optimizing Search Costs – A Comparative Study of Three Systems to Find the Best One . . . or Two . . . or Three . . . ." *ONLINE*, Vol. 5, No. 2 (1981), p. 38-43.

Hoover, Ryan E. *The Library and Information Manager's Guide to Online Services*. White Plains, NY: Knowledge Industry Publications, 1980.

Hoover, Ryan E. "A Comparison of Three Commercial ONLINE Vendors." *ONLINE*, Vol. 3, No. 1 (1979), p. 12-21.

Langlois, M. C. "Online Information Systems; Comparison of COMPENDEX, INSPEC and NTIS Search Files via LMS/DIALOG, SDC/ORBIT and SDS/RECON." *Online Review*, Vol. 1, No. 3 (1977), p. 230-237.

Rouse, Sandra H. and Lannom, Laurence W. "Some Differences between Three Online Systems: Impact on Search Results." *Online Review*, Vol. 1, No. 2 (1977), p. 117-132.

Williams, Martha E. *Computer-Readable Data Bases — A Directory and Data Sourcebook.* Washington, DC: American Society for Information Science, 1979.

7

Vocabulary Control

Proper identification of descriptive elements in a record is the key to successful information retrieval. Whether it is a single printed handbook or a warehouse of digitalized documents, access is always granted if index terms are chosen wisely. Even in cases where every significant word in a record can be searched, the presence of spelling variations, synonyms, homographs, and the like require the search analyst to be word-conscious.

The purpose of this chapter is to identify various online and hard copy language-related search aids. With a basic understanding of each tool, and a healthy dose of hands-on experience, the search intermediary should be able to determine the most effective combination for performing a successful search.

Several aspects of vocabulary control are examined in this chapter. The historical overview serves to establish the place of information retrieval by subject in the traditional world of libraries. The next section is devoted to the definition of some basic terminology and standards for formulating a controlled vocabulary. The steps involved in the construction and use of a thesaurus (the structured compilation of controlled terms) are followed by some basic guidelines on how to read a thesaurus. The online thesaurus, the advantages and shortcomings of natural-language indexing and searching, the effects of vocabulary control on the recall and precision of a search, as well as some basic suggestions on the location and use of supplementary search aids complete this general survey.

THE PAST

Throughout the history of the printed word, manual methods of information retrieval have depended upon various accessioning, indexing, and classification schemes to guide the seeker of information to the desired document. As the number of documents in individual collections began to grow and the number of searchers increased, the tendency to allow the user to browse through the collection also increased.

Filing systems which favored compact storage in closed stacks gradually gave way to more standard and universally acceptable classification schemes which physically grouped all subject-related documents and encouraged public access. A non-intuitive single access point — such as document size or acquisition date — gave way to more meaningful, multi-point classification by author, title, and appropriate subject(s).

Collections continued to grow. Soon the realities of limited space, limited budgets, and an increasing backlog of cataloging forced the information managers to seek alternatives to accepted methods of information storage and retrieval. Fortunately, computers were a part of this vicious circle of advanced technology which was not only producing an ever-increasing number of documents to be cataloged and stored, but also provided an opportunity to explore new avenues in bringing information and people together.

As with each endeavor touched by computers in the mid-twentieth century, the librarians' reaction to automation was that it could replicate the manual cataloging system, adding only greater speed and efficiency. It has taken over twenty years of experimentation, hard work, speculation, and faith to arrive at the era of generally dependable and affordable online bibliographic information retrieval.

There are numerous sources which trace the history of vocabulary control and discuss the role of computers in the preparation and use of indexes and thesauri (1, 2, 3, 4).

Exhaustive coverage of the concepts, design, development, and use of various indexes and thesauri are presented by Lancaster in his definitive text, *Vocabulary Control for Information Retrieval* (5). Inasmuch as a basic understanding of the history and language of any field eases the learning process of the mechanics of that subject, the reader may wish to become familiar with some of the references noted. However, for the purposes of understanding this chapter, the following discussion of definitions and standards should suffice.

DEFINITIONS AND STANDARDS

The common understanding of a given topic is greatly enhanced when its terminology is well-defined. As one's knowledge of the universe expands, so does the symbolism with which one attempts to define that universe. Communication skills are largely dependent upon this common pool of symbols. The thesaurus is a structured representation of this symbolism.

A thesaurus is created to explore the interrelationships, commonalities, and boundaries of a given subject. It is used to bridge the gap between the writer and the reader, between the indexer and the searcher of information.

One of the first comprehensive attempts at establishing guidelines for the construction of a thesaurus was Project LEX. Under the auspices of the Department of Defense, this project produced the *Thesaurus of Engineering and Scientific Terms* (TEST) (6).

These guidelines were subsequently adopted for thesaurus construction by the Committee on Scientific and Technical Information (COSATI) of the Federal Council for Science and Technology which produced the *Guidelines for the Development of Information Retrieval Thesauri* (7). In turn, the results of this work combined with that of the Engineers Joint Council's *Thesaurus Rules and Conventions* (8) and UNESCO's *Guidelines for the Establishment and Development of Monolingual Scientific and Technical Thesauri for Information Retrieval* (9) formed the basis for the *Guidelines for Thesaurus Structure, Construction, and Use* (10) adopted by the American National Standards Institute (ANSI) in 1973. This chapter's descriptions and definitions of the structure and use of the thesaurus are based upon these ANSI standards.

ANSI defines a thesaurus as "a compilation of words and phrases showing synonymous, hierarchical, and other relationships and dependencies, the function of which is to provide a standardized vocabulary for information storage and retrieval" (11). Its purpose is to convert the authors' natural language into a common language which can be used to expedite the transfer of information from the author to the ultimate user.

This proposed standardization allows for greater ease in the transfer of knowledge within a given subject area as well as across subject areas. For example, the U.S. Department of Commerce National Technical Information Service publishes an *Energy Microthesaurus* in an attempt to rectify indexing shortcomings of its energy related reports caused by the use of five different vocabulary sources. The following notation appears in the introduction to this microthesaurus:

> "It is the purpose of this microthesaurus not only to act as a thesaurus of energy terms but also to show the relationships between . . . five different sets of indexing keywords. . . . Others wishing to produce an energy indexing vocabulary will find it possible to use these established energy terms so that some degree of standardization may be achieved between different data bases" (12).

This example also illustrates that a "micro" thesaurus is not necessarily limited to a narrow field but rather to a specific approach to a given topic. A microthesaurus is in fact developed by extracting and combining pertinent terminology and methodology from one or more established thesauri.

THESAURUS CONSTRUCTION

Considering that thesauri are constructed not only to aid the indexer in describing the contents of a document but also to assist the searcher in locating the same material, it becomes apparent that a proficient search analyst must have a working knowledge of the basic ground rules for building a standard thesaurus.

Often the best approach to learning the uses of a tool is to become familiar with its basic design. In the case of a thesaurus, three construction steps are always present: identification of individual concepts, selection of appropriate terminology, and determination of interrelationships among terms and concepts. A brief discussion of each of these elements follows.

Concept Identification

The two most conventional methods for gathering thesaurus terms are the review of sample documents on the subject to be indexed, and referral to subject specialists or established subject authority lists. A subject authority list is a compilation of terms based upon the consensus of the experts in a given subject area. The National Library of Medicine's Medical subject headings (MeSH) and the Library of Congress Subject Headings are two examples of well-established subject authorities.

In preparation for searching, the same two methods of gathering entry terms can be used. Not only is it possible to refer to a database's own thesaurus, but it is also advisable to consult subject specialists, specialized dictionaries, or subject authority lists as supplementary means for expanding one's basic knowledge of the field. This method can be especially useful in full-text or natural language searches where the retrieval system is capable of searching every significant word in an entire record and places no restrictions on the search terms to be entered into the system.

Term Selection

Upon final identification and selection of concepts, a list of synonyms and near-synonyms must be constructed for cross-reference purposes. The nature and extent of such cross-referencing is directly related to the complexity of the subject matter and how well-established the field may be.

The most important step, of course, is the actual selection of terms which will be used in the thesaurus. It is essential that such terms, whether made up of a single word or of multiple words, represent a single concept. The necessity for a single-concept restriction becomes apparent when one considers the broad spectrum of users with differing needs (and thus differing concept combinations) attempting to use a single system. The following term selection rules, based upon ANSI standards, are widely recognized as applicable to a majority of thesauri:

1. The most preferred terms are nouns (single nouns, noun phrases, or nouns with parenthetical qualifiers).
2. Verb forms should generally be avoided, unless absolutely essential in conveying the full concept of a noun.

3. The following factors should be taken into account before deciding whether to precoordinate the thesaurus terms (i.e., use multiple words to describe a specific concept), or to allow for post-coordination by the searcher (i.e., use single, more generic terms which can be combined with other single terms at the time of search to produce the desired specificity):

   a. the frequency with which the term will be used in indexing,
   b. the breadth of the subject being indexed,
   c. the total number of terms to be used in indexing a given document,
   d. limits on meanings of concepts,
   e. the frequency with which the end user is likely to select a given term, and
   f. the use of terms in printed indexes versus their use in computerized databases.

4. Availability of some adjectives in the thesaurus may be useful in building a multiple-word concept. Terms such as "offshore" or "automated" may be precoordinated with certain nouns to identify concepts which may appear frequently in a subject area.
5. The singular form of a noun may be used to describe processes (such as fluoridation), properties (such as conductivity), or unique things (such as metric systems, earth, or water). The plural form may be used to describe classes of things, such as stars or teeth. In cases where both the singular and the plural forms are used, the singular usually denotes a process (e.g., painting), while the plural will describe the objects (e.g., paintings).
6. The natural word order should be followed in multiple word entries. Cross-references from the inverted form should be given (e.g., Materials, refractory — see: Refractory materials).
7. The use of punctuation marks, abbreviated forms, and special nomenclature pose their own unique problems in the thesaurus. Although ANSI has provided certain guidelines in all of these areas, the special subject matter of certain databases dictates the need for deviating from these standards. In addition, the database loading procedures of various commercial

retrieval systems may impose another set of restrictions on the use of such punctuation marks and abbreviations.

The underlying premise in the above guidelines is that there is a perceived logic in the structure of our language; that there is a common bond in the way we approach the definition of our subject. The thesaurus is designed on the basis of this common bond.

From a searcher's point of view, familiarity with these guidelines can save much time in the use of various thesauri. Where no thesaurus exists, and the object is to prepare a list of search terms for a free-text search, these same guidelines can be used to form logical search strategies. Regardless of the sophistication of the retrieval system, the searcher's knowledge of the subject and its language preempts most other considerations.

Term Relationships

The first step in building term relationships is the process of defining the index term itself. It is generally assumed that all of the widely used definitions for a term (as they appear in general purpose dictionaries) are also applicable to that term as used in the context of a special purpose thesaurus. If this is not the case, further refinement of the definition must be provided through a "scope note," by the addition of a modifier (multi-word concept), or through a parenthetical qualifier.

A scope note or an explanatory note can be used to control overlap with another term, describe an uncommon definition, or exclude a possible meaning from the chosen term. It is also helpful in thesaurus maintenance by providing the historical background of a term as used in that thesaurus. This type of notation can be useful when conducting retrospective searches. Following are some examples of scope notes from various thesauri:

ACCELERATION

The process of progressing through the school grades at a rate faster than that of the average child.

From *Thesaurus of ERIC Descriptors*, 1977

ACCELERATION

(Use only for general subject and for applications

not elsewhere classifiable, and apply code 921 for mathematical aspects, code 931 for mechanics aspects. Otherwise use subheading – Acceleration under heading for application, and cross-reference to ACCELERATION)

From *Subject Headings for Engineering*, 1979

CARDIAC OUTPUT, LOW

note category: do not confuse with CARDIAC OUTPUT, a physiol[ogical] concept above; also called 'low cardiac output syndrome' so do not add SYNDROME

From *Medical Subject Headings*, 1981

CHECKS AND CHECKING ACCOUNTS

Term used as of April, 1975. For earlier material, see Banks and Banking.

From *The Information Bank Thesaurus*, 1977

Scope notes are not considered a part of the thesaurus term and are not used in the online term entry process. On the other hand, parenthetical qualifiers are an integral part of the thesaurus term and must be used in the exact format specified by the system in order to retrieve relevant materials. Such qualifiers appear immediately after a term, on the same line of type, and are enclosed in parentheses.

Parenthetical qualifiers generally consist of one or two words which clarify term ambiguities such as homographs, or elaborate on restricted meanings. In some thesauri this method may be used to denote that a term is a registered trademark. Some examples of parenthetical qualifiers are as follows:

LETTERS (ALPHABET)
LETTERS (CORRESPONDENCE)

CHARTERS (CONSTITUTION)
CHARTERS (CORPORATIONS)

XEROX (TRADEMARK)

BEARING (DIRECTION)
BEARING (MACHINE PART)

FAIR (MARKET)
FAIR (ATTRACTIVENESS)

As with other aspects of thesaurus construction, published documents and subject authorities are the two major resources for developing patterns of term relationships. The standard medium for communicating such relationships in a thesaurus is the cross-reference. Cross-references are used to denote three types of relationships between or among various thesaurus terms:

1. Hierarchical relationships. One term may be broader (BT) or narrower (NT) than certain other terms in the thesaurus. For Example,

   CHEMICAL ANALYSIS

   BT Chemical tests
   NT Microanalysis
   Neutron activation analysis
   Polarographic analysis
   Qualitative analysis

2. Non-hierarchical relationships. Synonyms and antonyms, preferred terms, preferred spelling, and references to single-concept multi-word terms are among a variety of cases where the indexer or searcher is referred from one term to another by means of a "USE" or "USED FOR" notation (generally abbreviated as USE and UF). For example,

   ABRASION
   USE WEAR OF MATERIALS

   CATALOGUES
   USE CATALOGS

   CHEMICAL ANALYSIS

   UF Analytical chemistry
   Chemical determination
   Composition measurement
   Determination (chemical)

3. Related term (RT) concepts. This is when one term is closely related to another without necessarily qualifying for a broader term/narrower term relationship, such as:

(A) near synonyms:

ATTRITION
RT DROPOUTS

MISTS
RT FOGS

(B) usage-interrelated terms:

AUDIO EQUIPMENT
RT VIDEO EQUIPMENT

OILS
RT LUBRICATION

(C) whole-part related terms:

ATTENTION
RT ATTENTION CONTROL
ATTENTION SPAN
CURIOSITY

ATTITUDES
RT ATTITUDE TESTS

(D) overlapping concepts:

AUDIENCE PARTICIPATION
RT GROUP RELATIONS

CRIME
RT COURTS

READING THE THESAURUS

The thesaurus is a reference tool, and reference tools are for occasional use, not to be read from cover to cover. Why, then, the topic of thesaurus reading? As with any other reference tool, the comfort of using the thesaurus comes with age and association. Thesauri are the essential tools of the searching profession. It is imperative for the searcher to become acquainted with the entire structure of the thesaurus, learn its idiosyncrasies, and feel comfortable with it before starting to search. In this way, online time will be spent more efficiently, the cost of a search will be kept to a minimum, and the searcher will have the satisfaction of being in control of the search outcome.

Each thesaurus starts with an introductory preface. Some are quite detailed, while others barely meet the information needs of the searcher. However, in most cases the following essential information is provided:

1. Description of the subject matter covered and the basic reason for the construction of the thesaurus (i.e., the information storage and retrieval system which required the building of the controlled vocabulary).
2. Description of term arrangement, which may take the form of one or a combination of the following:

    a. *Alphabetical*: terms are sequenced alphabetically, with term relationships marked after each term. Table 7.1 is an example of an alphabetically arranged thesaurus.
    b. *Hierarchical*: terms are arranged according to their general/specific relationships. This is sometimes referred to as a "genus/species" relationship. An example of an hierarchical display is depicted in Table 7.2.
    c. *Network display*: a combination of related terms and generic relationships, this arrangement aids the user in visualizing term relationships. The Euratom-Thesaurus (Part II) is an example of a network display (see Table 7.3).
    d. *Permuted display*: generally refers to a computer-generated alphabetically arranged list of all terms (other than articles, prepositions, and similar "insignificant" terms) which appear in the title (or other predetermined sections) of a record. Two common examples of the permuted index are Keyword In Context (KWIC) and Keyword Out of Context (KWOC).

        A KWIC index shows the alphabetized index terms as they appear within the body of the text. The following example shows two titles ("Education and Training for Online Systems" and "Planning a User Group Workshop") and the manner in which they would appear in a KWIC index:

	Education and Training for
Planning a User	Group Workshop
Education and Training for	Online Systems
	Planning a User Group Workshop
Education and Training for Online	Systems
Education and	Training for Online Systems
Planning a	User Group Workshop
Planning a User Group	Workshop

A KWOC index extracts the index terms for compilation in a separate alphabetized list which is displayed alongside a portion of the text containing each term. For example, the same terms appearing in the above illustration would be displayed as follows:

Education	Education and Training for Online Systems
Group	Planning a User Group Workshop
Online	Education and Training for Online Systems
Planning	Planning a User Group Workshop
Systems	Education and Training for Online Systems
Training	Education and Training for Online Systems
User	Planning a User Group Workshop
Workshop	Planning a User Group Workshop

Of course, the above examples are theoretical. In practice, and as it specifically relates to thesauri, the permuted index of the Thesaurus of Engineering and Scientific Terms illustrates the logic for such an arrangement. This permuted index is a computer-generated, alphabetized display of every significant single or multi-word term in the thesaurus. This arrangement, as shown in Table 7.4, tends to group generically related terms which may have been separated by the strictly alphabetical sequence of the main thesaurus.

e. *Specialized terms displays*: arranges special terms in a manner appropriate to the use of those terms by subject specialists. Such a list may be composed of geographical place names, chemical names or formulas, alloy designations, engineering materials, disease names, and the like.

f. *Synonym dictionaries*: lists the preferred terms in alphabetical order, followed by all synonyms and/or antonyms for each term.

3. Explanation of the sequencing method used. When spaces between words in multi-word terms are ignored in the sequencing procedure, the filing system is referred to as "letter-by-letter" sequencing. The following group of words are arranged letter-by-letter:

Paperback Books

Paper Bags

Paperboard

Paper Boxboard

Paper Box Machinery

When the spacing between words of a multi-word term is not ignored, the result is a word-by-word sequencing system. Under this rule, the same words shown above would be arranged as follows:

Paper Bags

Paper Box Machinery

Paper Boxboard

Paperback Books

Paperboard

Apart from reading the introductory pages of a thesaurus, it is helpful to glance through the contents and perhaps trace the term relationships for a single concept. The searcher should become familiar with the thesauri available. The more one knows about the thesaurus structure, the better the chances for a satisfactory online search.

TABLE 7.1
An example of an alphabetical term display (from Mestt, 1981).

CARDIAC OUTPUT, LOW
C14.280.148
note category: do not confuse with CARDIAC OUTPUT, a physiol concept above; also called 'low cardiac output syndrome' so do not add SYNDROME
80
X LOW CARDIAC OUTPUT

CARDIAC PACEMAKER, ARTIFICIAL see PACEMAKER, ARTIFICIAL
E7.858.82.748

CARDIAC PACING, ARTIFICIAL
E2.145 E4.752.376.170
do not use /util except by MeSH definition; do not use /instrum (= PACEMAKER, ARTIFICIAL)
78
see related
PACEMAKER, ARTIFICIAL
X PACING, CARDIAC, ARTIFICIAL
XR ELECTRIC STIMULATION

CARDIAC RUPTURE see HEART RUPTURE
C14.280.470

CARDIAC RUPTURE, TRAUMATIC see HEART INJURIES
C21.866.473 C21.866.891.375

CARDIAC STIMULANTS see CARDIOTONIC AGENTS
D18.222+

CARDIAC TAMPONADE
C14.280.155
compression of heart from pericardial effusion or hemopericardium

CARDIAC VOLUME
G9.330.612.330
only /drug eff /rad eff; STROKE VOLUME is also available
72(68)

CARDIOGRAPHY, IMPEDANCE
E1.145.569.240 E1.145.811.611.250
E1.725.528.250
NIM; do not use /util except by MeSH definition
(79)
see under PLETHYSMOGRAPHY, IMPEDANCE
X IMPEDANCE, TRANSTHORACIC
X PLETHYSMOGRAPHY, IMPEDANCE, TRANSTHORACIC

CARDIOLIPIN SYNTHETASE
D8.586.913.696.125
do not use /analogs
(75)
see under PHOSPHOTRANSFERASES

TABLE 7.2
An example of a hierarchical term display (From *Thesaurus of Engineering and Scientific Terms*, New York: Engineering Joint Council, 1967.)

CHEMICAL PROPERTIES
.Acidity
.Alkalinity
.Chemical reactivity
.Chlorinity
.pH
.Salinity
.Thermochemical properties
. .Heat of ablation
. .Heat of absorption
. .Heat of activation
. .Heat of adsorption
. .Heat of crystallization
. .Heat of mixing
. .Heat of reaction
. . .Calorific value
. . .Heat of combustion
. . .Heat of dissociation
. . .Heat of formation
. . . .Heat of hydration
. .Heat of solution
. .Heat of transformation
. .Latent heat
. . .Heat of fusion
. . .Heat of sublimation
. . .Heat of vaporization
.valence

TABLE 7.3
Euratom network display (Courtesy of the Commission of the European Communities).

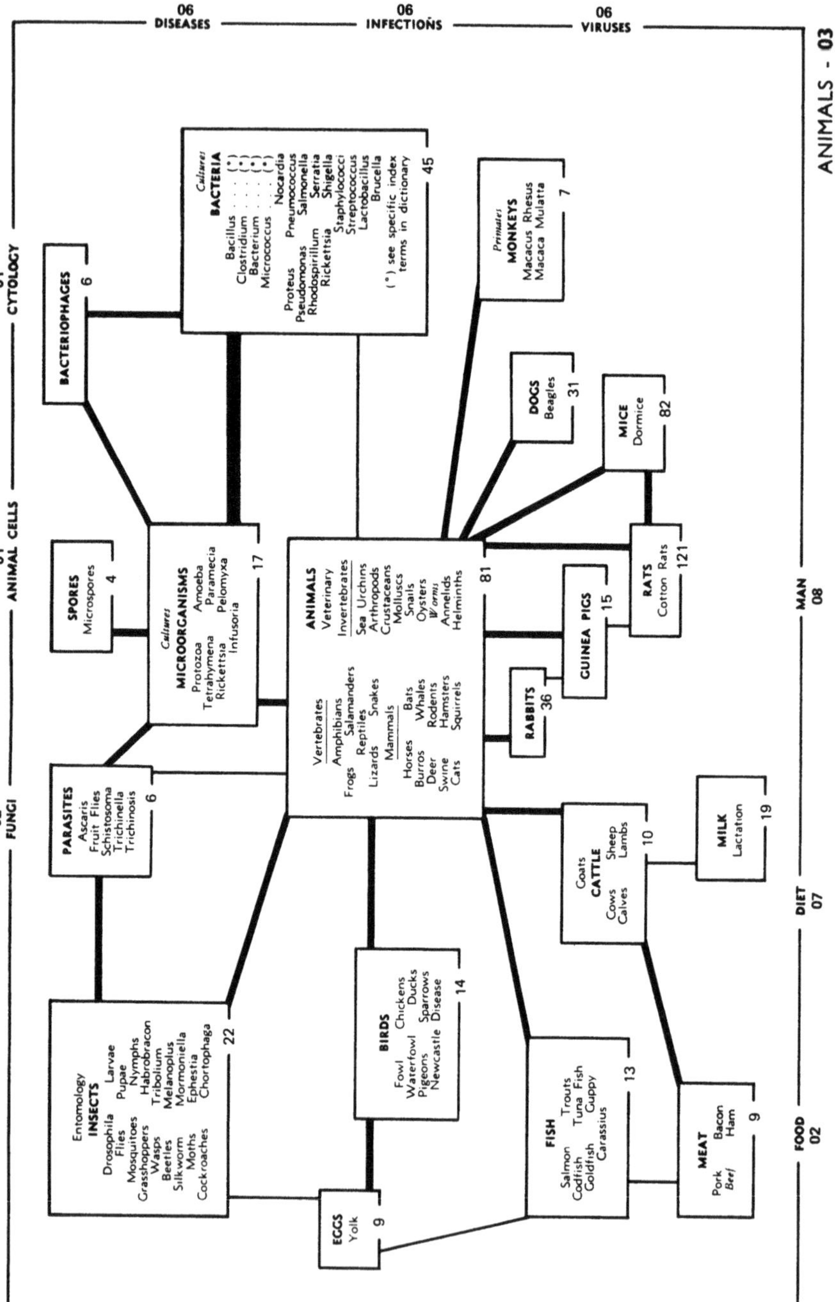

TABLE 7.4
An example of a permuted term display (From *Thesaurus of Engineering and Scientific Terms*, New York: Engineering Joint Council, 1967.)

BEARINGS
. Air bearings
Airframe bearings
Antifriction bearings
Ball bearings
Gas bearings
Jewel bearings
Journal bearings
Magnetic bearings
Needle bearings
Plain bearings
Radial bearings
Roller bearings
. Rolling contact bearings
Sleeve bearings
Taper roller bearings
Thrust bearings

(.) indicates USE reference

THE ONLINE THESAURUS

The online thesaurus can simply be the computer-readable form of a printed thesaurus, or it can be a modified or expanded version of the hard copy which has been partially or entirely generated with the aid of a computer program. Each database has its own unique system of utilizing the computer to cut down on the human effort necessary to keep a controlled vocabulary active and up-to-date.

The following is a small sample of various ways in which computer capabilities are used in the indexing process:

1. Triggered by the addition of an index term, the computer may automatically generate or add other terms from a predetermined list to complete a term relationship. Generally referred to as *autoposting*, this procedure assures a comprehensive coverage of general/specific, geographic, or time-related entries. For example, in the GEOREF thesaurus, if the index term APATITE is added to the thesaurus, the computer will

automatically add the mineral group PHOSPHATES as a broader term. Autoposted terms are clearly indicated in the thesaurus entry:

APATITE

BA	PHOSPHATES	("BA" indicates broader term autoposted)
BT	MINERALS	("BT" indicates broader term not autoposted)

2. Term history files can be maintained and updated by the computer. Obsolete and discarded terms can be tagged as such, and dates can be added automatically whenever new terms are stored.
3. The addition of new terms into a hierarchy, amendment of definitions, reconciliation of existing scope notes with changes in the language, and so on, can be instituted more readily and become immediately available to the users of the database.
4. An option may be provided to allow the indexers or users of the system to suggest new terms to be considered for future addition to the database. Such terms can be reviewed periodically for consideration as thesaurus entries.
5. Based on a human/computer cooperative system, the computer can match words from the natural-language text against a human-selected vocabulary of descriptors. Upon meeting certain conditions, or finding a perfect match, that term will be automatically assigned to the record. Other terms meeting a different set of criteria may be picked by the computer to appear on a list which can be reviewed by indexers for possible inclusion in the thesaurus.
6. The computer can, of course, be given full charge in automatically preparing an exhaustive index for the database. This index may be restricted to predetermined fields (such as a KWIC title index as described earlier in this chapter), or it may be based on entire records which are accessible in computer-readable form. Such an indexing procedure is described further in the next section.

NATURAL LANGUAGE INDEXING/SEARCHING

Natural language indexing or searching refers to the information retrieval system's capability to use the vocabulary of the authors of documents exactly as it appears in the body of the text. In other words, there is no fixed, indexer-based vocabulary to come between the system's searcher and the document's researcher or author.

In a database or retrieval system designed for natural language indexing, every significant word which appears in a searchable field (such as author, title, keywords, and abstract) becomes accessible as an index term. In fact, most systems exclude only a handful of "stop-words," or terms which are not indexed, such as "an," "and," "by," "for," "from," "of," "the," "to," and "with," from their exhaustive index.

Thus, a searcher using this database can freely choose from the general vocabulary of the indexed documents to access the online files. Although the natural language search is most amenable to the subject specialist who is well versed in the vocabulary of his or her field, it can also be a valuable tool for the search intermediary. In fact, one of the most significant causes of search failure in the natural language search – that of identifying every possible approach to the query – is less likely to hamper the experienced search analyst.

A lack of predetermined term relationships and the presence of all linguistic idiosyncracies lead to two other shortcomings in the natural language search: false coordinations and incorrect term relationships. The latter problem occurs when the searcher specifies the need for a combination of two or more terms, but finds that the records retrieved relate these terms in a manner inapplicable to the query. False coordination results when the terms occur in separate segments of the same record and bear no relationship to each other. Many advanced searching techniques, such as the use of truncation, adjacency commands, or assignment of term weights, have been devised to overcome the natural language search problems.

CONTROLLED VOCABULARY VS. THE FREE-TEXT SEARCH

Although the online vocabulary search aids are frequently more comprehensive and current than their hard copy counterparts, it is not always feasible to use these tools. When access time to the computer is limited (or the online system is not functioning), or search cost is an issue, or the search analyst has no previous experience with a given database, it is often wise to initiate the search process by reviewing the manual. Perusing the printed thesaurus is one of the most effective means of verifying the applicability of a given database to the information request.

One of the first steps in becoming familiar with a new database or search system is to determine the availability of all printed and online search aids, especially those related to vocabulary control. Many databases offer a printed thesaurus as well as an online vocabulary list which may be broader in scope and more up-to-date than its printed edition. Some databases offer only online thesauri based on the fact that keeping a printed thesaurus current can be prohibitively expensive.

In addition to the controlled vocabulary designated by individual databases (generally referred to as descriptors or index terms), each of the major information retrieval systems also provides a supplementary set of terms (or identifiers) for some databases, which can be used alone or in combination with the controlled vocabulary of the database. Another option offered by these systems is the free-text (uncontrolled vocabulary) searching of titles, abstracts, and subject fields of a database.

A combination of controlled and free-text searching is often the best approach in retrieving the greatest number of relevant citations in order to circumvent the inherent shortcomings of each medium. While the printed thesaurus offers a solid background in concept relationships, and the online thesaurus augments this tool, a free-text search allows the searcher to use the most recent terminology from the field and capture new topics and trends which may not be accepted at a level qualifying it for inclusion in the controlled vocabulary.

The starting point in term selection is, of course, the client's search request. The client may be very familiar with the field and be able to provide the appropriate terms. Whenever possible, the thesauri should be reviewed with the client to obtain his or her judgement of the appropriateness of each term for the desired concept.

It is also important to note that when a given database is available through a number of information retrieval systems, it is subject to the individual system's search program. Thus, the same basic information file may be manipulated in a variety of ways to produce different results (13).

A last caution, and one which is implicit in discussing the uniqueness of vocabulary structure for individual databases, is that a search strategy generally must be altered for use on different databases. A strategy which is tailored to the vocabulary of one database may not be at all appropriate for a database in a related field which has a different controlled vocabulary. There is less problem in transferring between uncontrolled vocabulary databases or in performing free-text searching on multiple databases, but the searcher still must be cautious in making the transition.

PRECISION AND RECALL

Defining an information request and assessing the client's expectations of the search system were discussed previously. The concepts of precision and recall as tools for evaluating system performance are discussed in more detail in Chapter 9. The following points stress the importance of vocabulary control in overall system performance:

1. If the broader terms have been autoposted, then the choice of broad, generic terms generally leads to greater recall (a greater number of records retrieved per search) and less precision (fewer number of relevant records retrieved per search). If the broader terms have not been autoposted, the use of broad terms may miss more specific items which are sought. The use of specific and/or complex terms produces greater precision but also may produce less recall unless the strategy is expanded to include synonyms, homographs, and closely related terms.
2. Lack of specificity and ambiguous relationships between terms are the two most common causes of search failures attributable to the vocabulary structure of a database.
3. If the search method is free-text (natural language), the searcher must rely upon personal knowledge of the field and experience with the database to formulate a logical search strategy. A natural language search is most likely to yield the highest precision in output. However, the lack of database control over such things as synonyms and homographs may result in a lower recall rate.

EXTERNAL/SUPPLEMENTARY SEARCH AIDS

Each database producer and search system vendor offers some basic vocabulary aids to the searcher. Such a service may range from an online, computer-generated index (or the ability to perform free-text searches) to a comprehensive mixture of printed and online thesauri and indexes.

Some databases or retrieval systems lacking a formal thesaurus provide online search aids which can improve the quality of search results. The use of all or part of strategies from previous searches conducted on the same system, a lookup of the term frequency data, citation searching, and reference to term history, are some of the ways in which the searcher can arrive at the right search strategy. Whenever such additional online tools are unavailable or inadequate, it is helpful to rely on external (supplementary) search aids to refine the search strategy. Apart from the supplier of the database itself, there are four major sources which provide additional search aids:

1. *Manual (hard copy) sources.* When the database thesaurus is inadequate or nonexistent, any or all of the following sources may be tapped for finding the appropriate terminology for the search at hand: suggestions from the client, current subject dictionaries, printed thesauri from other databases, indexes devised for manual search operations (most of which predate the online search systems), subject lists used in library cataloging, subject-related documents (especially in emerging subject fields), and special vocabulary tools designed for the specific subject of the query.
2. *Other database suppliers.* Other databases and their online or hard copy tools may be quite helpful in providing search hints which can have universal applications. For example, a single established thesaurus in a given field can serve as the authority list for that subject area. Thus, natural language databases can rely on the searcher's use of a pre-existing thesaurus to find reasonable access to the unindexed contents of their files.
3. *Commercial search systems.* These provide a wealth of additional search aids which can be used within or across the databases offered. At a primary level, all three major commercial information retrieval systems offer their own version of free-text searching as well as a basic (universal) index. Combined with the individual databases' controlled vocabulary, the Basic Index of SDC ORBIT or DIALOG or the Dictionary File of BRS

can be powerful tools in the information retrieval process. The advantages of a hybrid search system (combining controlled vocabulary with free-text search capabilities) have been well established.

4. *Other private firms and user groups.* Although user groups and private firms (such as library networks and regional training centers) emphasize other aspects of user training and do not generally provide vocabulary-related search aids, there is always ample opportunity for exchanging ideas and hints which encompass all aspects of the online search.

SUMMARY

Regardless of the type of database or retrieval system being used, the search intermediary must retain a certain level of control over the search vocabulary to obtain the desired results. The thesaurus is the most formal tool available to the searcher to exercise this option. When it is utilized in conjunction with the client's judgements and suggestions, it is a most effective tool. As described by Lancaster, "the thesaurus exists to lighten the intellectual burden on the searcher, to reduce the possibilities of human error, and to improve both the effectiveness and the cost-effectiveness of the search operation" (14).

The thesaurus also serves to reduce the reliance on human memory in identifying all terms which describe a concept.

To use a thesaurus effectively, it is important to become familiar with its structure as well as its content. It is also helpful to understand how the thesaurus – whether it is online or in hard copy format – is affected by the search capabilities of the retrieval system. For example, if the retrieval system offers truncation capabilities or automatic switching to the preferred listing of a term, the searcher can and should take advantage of these additional options.

EXERCISES

Assume that the following search requests were asked by a client. Select one or more databases for each search, each of which uses a controlled vocabulary.

For each request and each database selected, construct a search strategy using the appropriate thesaurus and any other vocabulary control tools required.

Perform the search online for each search request. For at least one of them, perform the search in two databases (using a customized strategy for each), and compare the retrieval.

For at least one question, perform a controlled vocabulary search and a free-text search on the same database and compare the retrieval.

1. Locate information on issues associated with nuclear reactor safety. The client is a technical expert but is preparing a speech for a local consumer group. Information from both the popular and scientific literature is needed.
2. Find articles which discuss strategic planning or long-range planning in the automotive industry.
3. Locate information on women in higher education (as administrators, teachers, or students).
4. Are there any references available on the use of computer-assisted instruction or personal computers in the high school classroom?
5. Identify articles on the use of art therapy or music therapy with patients who are schizophrenic or autistic. Do not include any articles which discuss patients with depression.

REFERENCES

1. Henderson, M. M. and others. *Cooperation, Convertibility, and Compatibility among Information Systems: A Literature Review*. Washington, DC: National Bureau of Standards, 1966.
2. Lancaster, F. W. "Vocabulary Control." *Encyclopedia of Library and Information Science*. New York: Marcel Dekker, 1969. Vol. 2.
3. Lancaster, F. W. *Information Retrieval Systems: Characteristics, Testing, and Evaluation*. 2nd ed. Los Angeles: Melville, 1979.
4. Vickery, B. C. "Thesaurus – A New Word in Documentation." *Journal of Documentation*, Vol. 16 (1960), p. 181-189.

5. Lancaster, F. W. *Vocabulary Control for Information Retrieval.* Washington, DC: Information Resources Press, 1972.
6. *Thesaurus of Engineering and Scientific Terms.* Revised ed. New York: Engineers Joint Council, 1967.
7. *Guidelines for the Development of Information Retrieval Thesauri.* U.S. Federal Council for Science and Technology, Committee on Scientific and Technical Information (COSATI). Washington, DC: Government Printing Office, 1967.
8. *Thesaurus Rules and Conventions.* New York: Engineers Joint Council, 1966.
9. *Guidelines for the Establishment and Development of Monolingual Scientific and Technical Thesauri for Information Retrieval.* Paris: United Nations Educational, Scientific and Cultural Organization, 1970.
10. *American National Standard Guidelines for Thesaurus Structure, Construction, and Use.* New York: ANSI, 1974.
11. *Ibid.*, p. 9.
12. *Energy Microthesaurus; A Hierarchical List of Indexing Terms Used by NTIS.* Springfield, VA: National Technical Information Service, 1976, p. iv.
13. Hoover, Ryan E. "A Comparison of Three Commercial ONLINE Vendors." *ONLINE*, Vol. 3, No. 1 (1979), p. 12-21.
14. Lancaster, F. W. *Vocabulary Control for Information Retrieval*, p. 189.

BIBLIOGRAPHY

American National Standard Guidelines for Thesaurus Structure, Construction, and Use. New York: ANSI, 1974.

Energy Microthesaurus; A Hierarchical List of Indexing Terms Used by NTIS. Springfield, VA: National Technical Information Service, 1976.

Guidelines for the Development of Information Retrieval Thesauri. U.S. Federal Council for Science and Technology, Committee on Scientific and Technical Information (COSATI). Washington, DC: Government Printing Office, 1967.

Guidelines for the Establishment and Development of Monolingual Scientific and Technical Thesauri for Information Retrieval. Paris: United Nations Educational, Scientific and Cultural Organization, 1970.

Henderson, M. M. and others. *Cooperation, Convertibility, and Compatibility among Information Systems: A Literature Review.* Wasington, DC: National Bureau of Standards, 1966.

Hoover, Ryan E. "A Comparison of Three Commercial ONLINE Vendors." *ONLINE*, Vol. 3, No. 1 (January, 1979), p. 12-21.

Lancaster, F. W. "Vocabulary Control." *Encyclopedia of Library and Information Science*. New York: Marcel Dekker, 1969. Vol. 2.

Lancaster, F. W. *Information Retrieval Systems: Characteristics, Testing, and Evaluation*. 2nd ed. Los Angeles: Melville, 1979.

Lancaster, F. W. *Vocabulary Control for Information Retrieval*. Wasington, DC: Information Resources Press, 1972.

Thesaurus Rules and Conventions. New York: Engineers Joint Council, 1966.

Vickery, B. C. "Thesaurus – A New Word in Documentation." *Journal of Documentation*, Vol. 16 (1960), p. 181-189.

8

Advanced Searching Techniques

In Chapter 5, the basic steps in the process of conducting an on-line search were outlined for the beginning searcher. The purpose of this chapter is to explore further the steps in the preparation and execution of the search strategy and to demonstrate some of the more sophisticated capabilities offered by the search system vendors and database suppliers. Presented here are some "tricks of the trade" – techniques to improve both the quality and speed of retrieval.

This chapter will address four broad categories of searching:

1. author searching
2. subject searching
3. searching for information from other fields
4. customizing and time-saving techniques

While some search capabilities are applicable to more than one category of searching, these four categories will provide a framework for the presentation of the techniques.

Many sample searches are included in this chapter and it would be repetitive to demonstrate all capabilities on each retrieval system. The search system on which each search was performed is identified. Many of the searching techniques are available from all three of the major commercial systems; where differences occur they will be noted. The reader is reminded that search system software is upgraded frequently, and specific capabilities and commands shown here may no longer be in use. Therefore, all system commands in these examples should be verified in system reference manuals before being used online.

UNIT RECORDS

Before discussing specific techniques, it is useful to review briefly the concept of the "unit record." The *unit record* is composed

```
ENTER BRS PASSWORD
MMMMMMMMM-I-S PASSWORD
MMMMMMMMM

03 MESSAGES PENDING IN MSGS
ACCESS VIA TELENET

BROADCAST MESSAGE CHANGED 05/24/83 AT 14:58:37.
ENTER 'Y' OR 'N' FOR BROADCAST MESSAGE._:    n
ENTER DATA BASE NAME_:    ntis

+SIGN-ON   14.38.13              5/25/83:

BRS/NTIS/1970 - JUL 1983

BRS - SEARCH MODE  - ENTER QUERY
    1_:    health adj systems adj agencies.ti.
    RESULT      74

    2_:    ..print 1 all/doc=1
     1
AN PB83-172700.
AU PUSKIN, DENA S.  LEE, EMMA K.  KACHMARYK, SUEANN.  SEGELMAN, SUSANNE.

IN FINGER LAKES HEALTH SYSTEMS AGENCY, ROCHESTER, NY. NATIONAL CENTER
   FOR HEALTH SERVICES RESEARCH, HYATTSVILLE, MD.  062314000.
TI DEVELOPMENT AND USE OF EXPENDITURE DATA FOR HSAS (HEALTH SYSTEMS
   AGENCIES). EXECUTIVE SUMMARY AND FINAL REPORT.
NT REPT. FOR 30 SEP 78-30 JUN 80.
YR 82.
```

Figure 8.1 Sample NTIS unit record on BRS.

```
   333P.
JN U8312.
SN NCHSR-83-3..
RN F.
CN PHS-HS-03459.
PR PC A15/MF A01.
CC 6E 44Q.
MN PAYMENT, NEW-YORK, EXPENSES, DATA-SOURCES, DEVELOPMENT, MEDICARE,
   PATIENTS, COMPARISON.
ID EXPENDITURES, HEALTH-CARE, COST-CONTAINMENT, HEALTH-PLANNING,
   HEALTH-SYSTEMS-AGENCIES, HEALTH-PLANNING-AGENCIES, NTISHRAHSR.
AB PREVIOUS ATTEMPTS TO DEVELOP EXPENDITURE PROFILES AT A LOCAL LEVEL
   WERE BASED ON PAYMENTS TO PROVIDERS IN AN AREA.  THESE EFFORTS DID
   NOT CONSIDER THE MIGRATION OF PATIENTS ACROSS GEOGRAPHIC BOUNDARIES
   AND HENCE COULD NOT PROVIDE AN ACCURATE MEASURE OF EXPENDITURES BY AN
   AREA'S RESIDENTS.  FEDERAL AND STATE EFFORTS ARE OFTEN LIMITED TO
   RELATIVELY LARGE REGIONS (E.G. STATE, HSA OR PSRO REGIONS), AND DO
   NOT PROVIDE IMPORTANT INTRAREGIONAL EXPENDITURE COMPARISONS.  THIS
   REPORT DESCRIBES THE DEVELOPMENT AND USE OF EXPENDITURE PROFILES IN A
   NINE-COUNTY UPSTATE NEW YORK REGION BASED ON COUNTY OF PATIENT
   RESIDENCE, IRRESPECTIVE OF WHERE CARE WAS RENDERED.  ESTIMATES OF A
   WIDE VARIETY OF HEALTH EXPENDITURES WERE DERIVED FROM SECONDARY DATA
   SOURCES.  TECHNIQUES WERE DEVELOPED TO TRANSLATE PROVIDER SPECIFIC
   DATA INTO RESIDENCE SPECIFIC DATA.  IN THE REPORT, METHODOLOGICAL AND
   PRAGMATIC RECOMMENDATIONS ARE SUMMARIZED REGARDING THE FUTURE CONDUCT
   OF SIMILAR SMALL AREA EXPENDITURES STUDIES.  THIS WORK HAS SHOWN THAT
   IT IS BOTH USEFUL AND FEASIBLE TO DEVELOP SMALL AREA EXPENDITURE
   PROFILES.  WHILE A PRIMARY OBJECTIVE OF THIS STUDY WAS TO EXPLORE THE
   USES OF EXPENDITURES DATA IN HEALTH PLANNING, THE LESSONS LEARNED
   SHOULD BE OF INTEREST TO OTHERS CONCERNED WITH THE DEVELOPMENT OF
   COST CONTAINMENT STRATEGIES.
```

Figure 8.1 (continued)

of individual data elements (also known as "fields"), such as author, title, descriptors (index terms), and abstract. Each unit record represents the total amount of data in the database describing one document or item. When an item is retrieved from a database, it is commonly referred to as a "record," "reference," or "citation," whether or not it contains all the information in the unit record.

The item represented by the unit record may be a book or a journal article in a bibliographic database, or a chemical or research project in a nonbibliographic database, for example. Figures 8.1 and 8.2 are samples of unit records from a bibliographic database, NTIS (National Technical Information Service), and from a nonbibliographic database, Chemname (a chemical dictionary).

It is important to recognize that not all databases contain the same fields in their unit records, nor even the same abbreviations

```
ENTER YOUR DIALOG PASSWORD
MMMMMMMMM  LOGON FILE1 WED 25MAY83 14:05:04 PORT070


++ FILE 17 IS UNAVAILABLE ON TELENET
++     FILE 36 IS NOT WORKING
?news news:
   +NEW IMPROVED TYMNET NOW AVAILABLE+
  FREE TIME OFFER IN MAY:
   ENVIRONMENTAL BIBLIOGRAPHY (#68)
  NOW AVAILABLE:
   UPI NEWS (FILE 261)
   CHEMICAL EXPOSURE (FILE 138)
  ANNOUNCEMENTS:
   PRICE CHANGE FOR COFFEELINE (#164)
? b31
          25MAY83 14:05:31 USER2549
   $0.23  0.009 HRS FILE1+
   $0.07  TELENET
   $0.30  ESTIMATED TOTAL COST

FILE31:CHEMNAME(TM) 1967-JUN82 1,279,331 SUBS
(COPR. DIALOG INF.SER.INC.1983)
         SET ITEMS DESCRIPTION
         --- ----- -----------

? s hexachlorobenzene
           1      9 HEXACHLOROBENZENE
? type1/5/1
1/5/1
    CAS REGISTRY NUMBER:  51568-42-4
    FORMULA: C6H12N2S4.06H60L6.060L6
    ANALYSIS OF RINGS: 06
    NUMBER OF RINGS: 1
    SIZE OF RINGS: 6
    CA NAME(S):
    HP=THIOPEROXYDICARBONIC DIAMIDE(((H2N)0(S))2S2) (90I), SB=TETRAMETHYL-,
NM=MIXT. WITH HEXACHLOROBENZENE AND (1.ALPHA.,2.ALPHA.,3.BETA.,
4.ALPHA.,5.ALPHA.,6.BETA.)-1,2,3,4,5,6-HEXACHLOROCYCLOHEXANE
    SYNONYMS:  PEI 121; THIRAHEXALIN
    OTHER CA NAMES:
    HP=BENZENE (90I), SB=HEXACHLORO-, NM=MIXT. CONTG.
    HP=CYCLOHEXANE (90I), SB=1,2,3,4,5,6-HEXACHLORO_, NM=(1.ALPHA.,2.ALPHA-
 .,3.BETA.,4.ALPHA.,5.ALPHA.,6.BETA.)-, MIXT. CONTG.

? logoff
          25MAY83 14:07:02 USER2549
    $3.73  0.027 HRS FILE31 1 DESCRIPTOR
    $0.22  TELENET
    $0.12  1 TYPES
    $4.07  ESTIMATED TOTAL COST


LOGOFF 14:07:11

415 48 DISCONNECTED
```

Figure 8.2 Sample Chemname unit record on DIALOG.

for the field when the content is the same. (These field abbreviations are known as "mnemonics.") In addition, not all fields are searchable, i.e., one cannot request the computer to retrieve all items in French if language is not a searchable field in the database. Consequently, it is possible to have searchable-only fields, printable-only fields, and fields that are both searchable and printable. Printable fields are those which can be displayed at the searcher's request.

Search system vendor and database producer reference manuals must be consulted to determine the status of individual fields in a particular database and the way they are coded on that particular search system. The following fields are both searchable and printable in most bibliographic databases:

- author
- title
- journal citation
- year of publication
- language
- subject terms (whether free-text or from a controlled vocabulary)

AUTHOR SEARCHING

Author Name Format

Nearly all bibliographic databases allow the searcher to retrieve items by author. Before attempting to do so, the appropriate database manual should be consulted to determine the rules governing the input of authors' names. For example, is access provided to all authors of a document, only the first three authors, or only to the first author listed? Thus, if a database provides access only to the first author, it will not be possible to identify works by an individual when that person was a co-author.

The searcher must also determine the exact format that was used to enter the authors' names into the database. For instance, some databases input all authors as last name first, followed by initials (e.g., Smith JP). Other databases may use the full first name of the author (e.g., Smith Jane P). Variations exist in the form of punctuation, such as whether to put a comma after the surname. Because the computer matches on a character-by-character basis, the format of the search term must be precisely the same as the format in the database in order for a match to occur.

```
FILE55:BIOSIS PREVIEWS - 1977 THRU 1980
(COPR. BIOSIS 1980)
SEE FILES 5.255
         SET ITEMS DESCRIPTION
         --- ----- -----------

? e au=krook l
REF ITEMS  INDEX-TERM
E1      1  AU=KROOK J
E2      2  AU=KROOK J M
E3     26 +AU=KROOK L            (Note the possible inconsistent
E4      3  AU=KROOK L P           use of the middle initial)
E5      5  AU=KROOK P M
E6      3  AU=KROON A
E7     19  AU=KROON A M
E8      1  AU=KROON C C M        (Unless middle initial is known,
E9      2  AU=KROON D J           both versions of the name must
E10     1  AU=KROON F             be selected for thoroughness)
E11     1  AU=KROON F H M
E12     3  AU=KROON G H

                           -MORE-
? s e3-e4
           1    29 E3-E4
                   E3: AU=KROOK L
?
```

Figure 8.3 BIOSIS previews on DIALOG.

In some databases the author name format will be unstandardized; the name will be entered exactly as it appears in the document. If unstandardized, it is not unusual for an author's name to appear in multiple forms within the same database. For example, Jane Smith may appear in one database in all of these forms:

- Smith J
- Smith, J.P.
- Smith Jane P
- Smith Jane Paula

Ignoring the rules of input can drastically affect one's retrieval when performing an author search. These types of differences are the result of the methods used to create the database by the producers, not the way in which it is processed by the search system vendors.

```
FILE72:EXCERPTA MEDICA - 1980-83/ISS05
COPR. ESP BY/EXCERPTA MEDICA 1983
         SET ITEMS DESCRIPTION
         ___ _____ ___________

? e au=krook l
REF ITEMS  INDEX-TERM
E1      1  AU=KROOK J.E.
E2      2  AU=KROOK J.M.
E3        +AU=KROOK L
E4      7  AU=KROOK L.
E5      1  AU=KROOK L.P.     (Note use of periods after initials.)
E6      3  AU=KROOK P.M.
E7      1  AU=KROON A.G.
E8      6  AU=KROON A.M.
E9      4  AU=KROON B.B.R.
E10     1  AU=KROON C.
E11     1  AU=KROON C.C.M.
E12     1  AU=KROON D.J.
                               -MORE-
? s e4-e5
          1     8 E4-E5
                   E3: AU=KROOK L

?
```

Figure 8.4 Excerpta Medica on DIALOG.

Identify All Forms of Author Name

In addition to consulting the proper manuals, many searchers follow this rule of thumb when performing author searches: always "expand" (also known as "neighbor" or "root") on an author's name in a database to check spelling and input format before searching.

The concept known as "expanding" in DIALOG, "neighboring" in SDC, and "rooting" in BRS, refers to the process of consulting an index within the database. Two indexes are most commonly consulted: the author index and the subject index (also called "basic index"). This command allows the searcher to view, in alphabetical order, a series of entry points. In some databases, both indexes are integrated into one and viewed simultaneously. Figures 8.3, 8.4, and 8.5 exemplify an expansion of an author's name (L. Krook) on each of three databases. Note that the name is searchable in several different ways and failure to include each format in the search strategy would result in an incomplete author search.

```
FILE6:NTIS - 64-83/ISS14
(COPR. NTIS)
        SET ITEMS DESCRIPTION
        --- ----- -----------

? e au=krook l
REF ITEMS  INDEX-TERM
E1     12  AU=KROO, N.
E2      3  AU=KROODSMA, R. L.
E3        +AU=KROOK L
E4      2  AU=KROOK, L. O.       (Note use of both initials and
E5      2  AU=KROOK, M.           full first names in this file.)
E6      1  AU=KROOK, R.
E7      1  AU=KROON, D. H.
E8      3  AU=KROON, I.
E9      2  AU=KROON, J. C.
E10     5  AU=KROON, J. J.
E11     1  AU=KROON, JOHANNES
              JOSEPH
                                       -MORE-
? s e4
           1      2 AU=KROOK, L. O.
? b94
```

Figure 8.5 NTIS on DIALOG.

On DIALOG and BRS, one may select a sequential series of entry formats from the expansion so that it is not necessary to re-enter each form of the author's name separately. Note also that the expansion provides the number of entries (or "hits") in the database for each form of the author's name.

Truncation

Another mechanism which allows for variations in an author's name is "truncation." *Truncation* refers to the ability to request all forms of entry which include a specified series of characters. The character string is entered, followed by a truncation symbol. In the SDC system, a colon is used. Thus, "Levinson S:" would retrieve any author with a surname of Levinson and any form of first name beginning with "S," such as "Shirley" or "Stephen," regardless of any middle name or initial. Truncation can be applied to other fields as well.

Citation Searching

Two databases, Science Citation Index and Social Science Citation Index, allow the searcher to retrieve documents which *cite* a particular work authored by a given individual. For example, if J.P. Guilford published an article in 1962, it would be possible to determine how many times (and by whom) it has been referenced in recent years. Citation searching is useful for identifying works in a limited subject area, based on the assumption that authors working in the area will cite a classic earlier work. It is also useful in searching topics that cross several subject areas in which different vocabulary terms apply. One can identify records based on known authors working in the field rather than using subject terms that may be imprecise in describing the topic.

When performing citation searching, it is helpful to have a complete reference to the cited article. Expanding on the author name is one way to determine the form of the citation in the database. Notice that the citations are entered as they are found and that variant forms may be stored in the database. Figure 8.6 illustrates a search for any references to the author, "J.P. Guilford."

SUBJECT SEARCHING

In discussing subject searching, it is necessary to distinguish between free-text and controlled vocabulary searching. Free-text searching utilizes every significant word in the title, the abstract, and other designated searchable fields. Controlled vocabulary searching limits the retrieval to index terms (or descriptors) which have been assigned to the record.

Adjacency Searching

The concept of adjacency is important when searching in a free-text mode. *Adjacency* refers to the ability to specify that two or more words appear in a particular relationship, such as next to each other in a specified order or with some maximum number of intervening words. Its use reduces the problem of "false drops" (irrelevant retrieval). The adjacency capability is illustrated in figure 8.7.

This search was performed on the ERIC database using the BRS system. The BRS adjacency operator, "ADJ," demonstrates

```
FILE186:SCISEARCH - 74-77
(COPR. ISI INC.)
SEE ALSO FILES 34 AND 94
         SET ITEMS DESCRIPTION
         --- ----- -----------

? e cr=guilford jp, 1962
REF ITEMS  INDEX-TERM
E1      2  CR=GUILFORD JP, 1961
E2      1  CR=GUILFORD JP, 1961
             V68, P1
E3      3 +CR=GUILFORD JP, 1962
E4      1  CR=GUILFORD JP, 1962,
             P151
E5      1  CR=GUILFORD JP, 1962,
             V22, P439
E6      1  CR=GUILFORD JP, 1962,
             V6, P87
E7      2  CR=GUILFORD JP, 1962,
             V63, P380
                           -MORE-

? p
REF ITEMS  INDEX-TERM
E8      1  CR=GUILFORD JP, 1963
E9      1  CR=GUILFORD JP, 1963,
             P101
E10     1  CR=GUILFORD JP, 1963,
             V60, P269
E11    10  CR=GUILFORD JP, 1964
E12    99  CR=GUILFORD JP, 1965
E13     1  CR=GUILFORD JP, 1965,
             PCH11
E14     1  CR=GUILFORD JP, 1965,
             P185
                           -MORE-
? s e3,e7
          1      5 E3,E7
                 E3: CR=GUILFORD JP, 1962
?
```

(CR=Cited Reference)

(Selection of CR=Guilford JP? would retrieve all articles in the file which cite any work by Guilford because the use of the truncation symbol [?] allows for all variables. Expansion was done to identify and select only those articles which cite a particular 1962 work.)

(Article to be searched appeared in Vol. 63 of a journal and began on pg. 380.)

(NOTE: For thoroughness, both forms of entry must be selected as some authors may have cited only author and year.)

(Note also the ability to select entries from the expansion and separate by commas.)

Figure 8.6 SCISEARCH on DIALOG.

```
BRS - SEARCH MODE - ENTER QUERY
    1_:   higher and education        (Two singly searched free-text
    RESULT    82498                    words which must appear
                                       somewhere in the same unit
                                       record.)

    2_:   higher adj education        (Two words must appear side
    RESULT    77240                    by side anywhere in unit
                                       records, including titles,
                                       abstracts or subject
                                       headings.)

    3_:   higher-education            (Use of subject heading
    RESULT    73995                    [descriptor or index term]
                                       from ERIC thesaurus.
                                       Note that two word subject
    4_:   ..off                        headings are input into BRS
                                       separated by hyphen.)

+CONNECT TIME  0:01:52 HH:MM:SS   0.031 DEC HRS  SESSION  1343+

EST ERIC COST:  C-HRS  DB-ROY  CIT-ROY  COMM   TOTAL

                 $.50   $.00     $.00    $.22   $.72

+SIGN-OFF  14.
```

Figure 8.7 ERIC on BRS.

the different number of records retrieved with "higher ADJ education" as compared to "higher AND education." In some systems it is also possible to specify that the terms be within a certain distance from each other (SDC calls this "proximity searching"). For instance, in DIALOG, adjacency is represented by "(W)." If one wishes the word "future" to fall within three words of "planning," the phrase would be input as "future(3W)planning." For further variations on the use of adjacency, consult the system reference manuals.

Restricting a Search to Specified Fields

It is possible to "qualify" or explicitly designate the field in which the adjacent words are to appear. For example, in order to retrieve records with "strategic planning" in their titles, the following phrases would be entered on the three systems:

```
PLEASE TYPE YOUR TERMINAL I
-2435:01-027-
PLEASE LOG IN:  sdc

PASSWORD:

REMOTE: CALL CONNECTED
/login sdcpgsph

YOU ARE ON LINE L96

HELLO FROM SDC/ORBIT IV.  (05/25/83  12:30 P.M.  PACIFIC TIME)
ENTER SECURITY CODE:
MMMMMMMMMM


PROG:
++++
FEDREG, CRECORD NOW HAVE SDI SERVICE! SEE NEWS.
++++
YOU ARE NOW CONNECTED TO THE ORBIT DATABASE.
FOR A TUTORIAL, ENTER A QUESTION MARK.  OTHERWISE, ENTER A COMMAND.

USER:
file enviroline

PROG:
ELAPSED TIME ON ORBIT: 0.01 HRS.
YOU ARE NOW CONNECTED TO THE ENVIROLINE DATABASE.
COVERS 1971 THRU JAN (8301)


SS 1 /C?
USER:
radon


PROG:
SS 1 PSTG (215)            (Free-text occurrence of word.)


SS 2 /C?
USER
radon/it


PROG:
SS 2 PSTG (189)      (Use of word as a descriptor or index term.)


SS 3 /C?
USER:
```

Figure 8.8 Environline on SDC.

System	*Phrase*
DIALOG	strategic(w)planning/ti
SDC	strs/ti :strategic(w)planning
BRS	strategic adj planning.ti.

Qualifying is also useful for limiting single word descriptor terms to their occurrence in the descriptor or index term field. This avoids false drops which may be retrieved by the free-text occurrence of the single word in a title or abstract. In most cases, limitation of the search to descriptors results in more relevant retrieval than free-text searching. Figure 8.8 illustrates the difference in retrieval for "radon" as a descriptor vs. "radon" as a free-text occurrence in the Enviroline database.

```
ENTER BRS PASSWORD
MMMMMMMMM-I-S PASSWORD
MMMMMMMMMMM
03 MESSAGES PENDING IN MSGS

ACCESS VIA TELENET

BROADCAST MESSAGE CHANGED 05/27/83 AT 14:28:04.
ENTER 'Y' OR 'N' FOR BROADCAST MESSAGE._:      n
ENTER DATA BASE NAME_:   psyc

+SIGN-ON    16.08.43            5/27/83:

BRS/PSYC/1967 - APR 1983

BRS - SEARCH MODE - ENTER QUERY
    1_:     root marriage
        MARRIAGE$
R1      MARRIAGE                                    3748 DOCUMENTS
R2      MARRIAGE-ATTITUDES                           238 DOCUMENTS
R3      MARRIAGE-COUNSELING                          752 DOCUMENTS
R4      MARRIAGE-RITES                                15 DOCUMENTS
R5      MARRIAGEABILITY                                1 DOCUMENT
R6      MARRIAGEABLE                                   4 DOCUMENTS
R7      MARRIAGES                                    445 DOCUMENTS

    1_:     marriage.mj.                       (Word "marriage" limited
    RESULT      823                             to single word descriptor.)
```

Figure 8.9 Psychological Abstracts on BRS.

```
FILE172:EXCERPTA MEDICA - 1975 thru 1979
 (COPR.  EM)
SEE FILES 72,73
         SET ITEMS DESCRIPTION
         ___ _____ ___________

  e abortion
REF  ITEMS INDEX-TERM              RT
E1       1 ABORTIFAVIENT
E2       1 ABORTIFICIENTS
E3       1 ABORTIGENIC
E4      15 ABORTINDUKTION
E5      49 ABORTING
E6    5335+ABORTION  DC=0000100    9
E7         ABORTION ACT            1
E8         ABORTION AGENT          1
E9       1 ABORTION BLOOD
E10      1 ABORTION CANNULA
E11      1 ABORTION CENTRE
E12      1 ABORTION CLINICS
E13      1 ABORTION COMMITTEE
E14      1 ABORTION COMPLICATION
                DC=0157757
E15      1 ABORTION COMPLICATIONS
E16      1 ABORTION DATA
E17        ABORTION DRUG           1
E18      1 ABORTION IN 21TH WEEK
E19      1 ABORTION INDICATION
                              -MORE-
? e e8
REF  ITEMS INDEX-TERM              RT
E1         ABORTION AGENT          1
E2      16 ABORTIVE
             AGENT DC=0080974      6
```

(DC number denotes index term.)

(Postings in related terms field [RT] lead searcher to proper descriptor for that concept through second expansion)

(Postings in items field indicate number of references on database in which that word or term appears.)

Figure 8.10 Excerpta Medica on DIALOG.

Identifying All Forms of the Term

The "expand" capability applies to the subject index as well as to the author name index. Figure 8.9 illustrates the subject term expansion capability on BRS. It is important to note the difference in postings for the single word in the expansion and the same word qualified to the descriptor field.

In some databases, the expand capability will allow the searcher to learn which words and phrases are descriptors as well as what terms can be found for free-text searching. Figure 8.10 illustrates the use of "expand" for this purpose on the database Excerpta Medica.

Truncation

Truncation is often used in subject searching as well as author searching. For example, truncating the character string "pregnan" will retrieve "pregnancy," "pregnancies," or "pregnant." The character string would be entered on the three major search systems as follows:

System	*Form of Entry*
DIALOG	S pregnan?
SDC	all pregnan:
BRS	pregnan$

It is usually possible to qualify a truncated series of characters to a single field. The above search string can be limited to the title field in the following manner:

System	*Form of Entry*
DIALOG	S pregnan?/ti
SDC	all pregnan:/ti
BRS	pregnan?.ti.

Subject term truncation is illustrated in Figure 8.11.

OTHER SEARCHABLE FIELDS

Some searches will be for information other than author or subject. This is especially true in nonbibliographic databases where a specific piece of information may be sought. For example, using a chemical dictionary file such as Chemname or Chemdex, one may wish to retrieve factual information on the chemical whose molecular formula is C7H5NO3S and whose common name is saccharin. The appropriate data elements can be searched as illustrated in Figure 8.12. Fields other than the title may be printed to provide specific factual information and to check for relevance.

There may be an occasion to search in the author address field, such as to determine all authors in France writing on heart transplantation. Similarly, in the SSIE database, one may wish to identify all projects which are currently being funded by the National Institutes of Mental Health. The searcher must ascertain which fields are searchable in the database selected and review

```
BRS/DISS/1861 - JUN 1983
                                                   (Search on recruitment and
BRS - SEARCH MODE  - ENTER QUERY                    retention of nurses.)
    1_:    nurs$3.ti.                              (Truncation of nurs
    RESULT     2826                                 to allow up to three
                                                    additional characters
                                                    [i.e., nurse, nurses, nursing]
                                                    qualified to appear in title
                                                    field.)
    2_:   recruit$ or retention or retain$ or turnover
    RESULT     2536                                ("Recruit" and "retain"
                                                    truncated so that any
                                                    ending to these words
                                                    is acceptable.)
    3_:    1 and 2
    RESULT       24

    4_:    ..print 3 ti/doc=1-5                    (Several titles viewed
     1                                              for relevance.)
TI THE RELATIONSHIP OF JUNGIAN PSYCHOLOGICAL TRAITS OF ASSOCIATE DEGREE
   NURSES TO RETENTION AND PREDICITON OF SUCCESS.

     2
TI FACTORS INFLUENCING RETENTION OF NEW NURSING GRADUATES IN HOSPITAL
   AND PROFESSIONAL PRACTICE.

     3
TI SOME FACTORS CONTRIBUTING TO RETENTION OF REGISTERED NURSES IN
   SELECTED KANSAS CITY AREA HOSPITALS.

     4
TI REDUCING NURSING TURNOVER: ORGANIZATIONAL LEARNING THROUGH ACTION
   TRAINING AND RESEARCH.

     5
TI EFFECTS OF TWO EDUCATIONAL METHODS UPON RETENTION OF KNOWLEDGE IN
   PHARMACOLOGY AND UPON JOB SATISFACTION AMONG STAFF NURSES.

            END OF DOCUMENTS
```

Figure 8.11 Dissertation Abstracts on BRS.

the rules of input for those fields. It may be necessary to determine if the country name is in the database, in which field it is stored, and how it is formatted. Assuming that the country name is searchable, are the names in full form or abbreviated? If they are abbreviated, what list of abbreviations is used?

```
FILE31:CHEMNAME(TM) 1967-JUNE82 1,279,331 SUBS
(COPR. DIALOG INF.SER.INC.1983)
        SET ITEMS DESCRIPTION
        --- ----- -----------

? s mf=c7h5no3s                        (Molecular formula searched and
          1    31 MF-C7H5NO3S           combined with free-text term.)
? s saccharin
          2    38 SACCHARIN
? ss s2 and s1
          3    13  2 AND 1
? type3/3/1-3
3/3/1
   CAS REGISTRY NUMBER: 17248-06-5
   FORMULA: C7H5NO3S.C2H7NO
   ANALYSIS OF RINGS: C3NS-C6
   NUMBER OF RINGS: 2
   SIZE OF RINGS: 5,6
   FORMULA OF RINGS: NSC3
   CA NAME(S):
   HP=1,2-BENZISOTHIAZOLIN-3-ONE (8CI),    NM-1,1-DIOXIDE,  COMPD.  WITH
2-AMINOETHANOL (1:1)
   HP=1,2-BENZISOTHIAZOL-3(2H)-ONE (9CI),  NM=1.1-DIOXIDE,  COMPD.  WITH
2-AMINOETHANOL (1:1)
   SYNONYMS: SACCHARIN COMPD. WITH ETHANOL AMINE

3/3/2
   CAS REGISTRY NUMBER: 17248-07-6
   FORMULA:  C7H5NO3S.C4H11NO2
   ANALYSIS OF RINGS: C3NS-C6
   NUMBER OF RINGS: 2
   SIZE OF RINGS: 5,6
   FORMULA OF RINGS: NSC3
   CA NAME(S):
   HP=1,2-BENZISOTHIAZOLIN-3-ONE  (8CI),  NM=1,1-DIOXIDE,  COMPD.  WITH
2.2/-IMINODIETHANOL  (1:1)
   HP=1,2-BENZISOTHIAZOL-3(2H)-ONE (9CI), NM=1,1-DIOXIDE,  COMPD.  WITH
2,2/-IMINOBIS(ETHANOL)  (1:1)
   SYNONYMS:   SACCHARIN  COMPD.   WITH DIETHANOL AMINE;  DIETHANOL
AMINESACCHARINATE
   OTHER CA NAMES:
   HP=ETHANOL (9CI), SB=2,2/-IMINOBIS-, NM=COMPD. WITH 1,2-BENZISOTHIAZOL-
-3(2H)-ONE 1,1-DIOXIDE (1:1)

3/3/3
  CAS REGISTRY NUMBER:  70142-21-1
  FORMULA: C7H5NO3S.LI
  ANALYSIS OF RINGS: C3NS-C6
  NUMBER OF RINGS: 2
  SIZE OF RINGS: 5,6
  FORMULA OF RINGS: NSC3
  CA NAME(S):
  HP=1,2-BENZISOTHIAZOL-3(2H)-ONE (9CI), NM=1,1-DIOXIDE, LITHIUM SALT
  SYNONYMS: SACCHARIN LITHIUM SALT

?
```

Figure 8.12 Chemname on DIALOG.

```
BRS/MESH/1979 - JUN 1983

BRS - SEARCH MODE  - ENTER QUERY
    1_:    health-policy.mj.
    RESULT      542

    2_:    ..limit/1lg=en                    (Retrieval limited to
    RESULT      469                           English language.)
```

Figure 8.13 MEDLINE on BRS.

CUSTOMIZING AND TIME SAVING TECHNIQUES

Customizing the Search to Client Requirements

Special techniques may be employed to increase the suitability of the retrieval to client requirements or to speed the completion of the search. Some techniques may be applied to customizing the results of the search. For example, if the client is interested only in items published within a certain time period, in many databases it is possible to restrict the retrieval by year of publication. Language is another element commonly used for restricting search results. For example, one may retrieve only those items which contain abstracts or those which fall into a given publication type, such as books, journal articles, or patents. Some databases allow the search output to be sorted in a specified order, such as alphabetically by author's name or journal title, before printing. Sorting is particularly useful if the output from more than one database can be merged in the sort. Figures 8.13, 8.14, and 8.15 demonstrate capabilities for restricting search results.

```
FILE172:EXCERPTA MEDICA - 1975 THRU 1979
 (COPR. EM)
SEE FILES 72,73
          SET ITEMS DESCRIPTION
          --- ----- -----------

? s laetrile
            1    66 LAETRILE
? limit1/abs                                (Retrieval limited
            2    16 1/ABS                   to references
                                            with abstracts.)
```

Figure 8.14 Excerpta Medica on DIALOG.

```
PROG:
++++
FEDREG, CRECORD NOW HAVE SDI SERVICE: SEE NEWS.
++++
YOU ARE NOW CONNECTED TO THE ORBIT DATABASE.
FOR A TUTORIAL, ENTER A QUESTION MARK.  OTHERWISE, ENTER A COMMAND.

USER:
file ntis

PROG:
ELAPSED TIME ON ORBIT: 0.01 HRS.
YOU ARE NOW CONNECTED TO THE NTIS DATABASE.
COVERS 1970 THRU V83 #13 (8313)

SS 1 /C?
USER:
interferon

PROG:
SS 1 PSTG (268)

SS 2 /C?
USER:                                    (Retrieval limited
1 and greater than 79                     in various ways
                                          by year of publication.)

PROG:
SS 2 PSTG (33)

SS 3 /C?
USER:
1 and from 77 thru 78

PROG:
SS 3 PSTG (41)

SS 4 /C?
USER:
1 and from 80-81

PROG:
SS 4 PSTG (24)

SS 5 /C?
USER:
stop
```

Figure 8.15 NTIS on SDC.

Techniques to Speed the Search Process

Search system vendors have instituted a number of search facilities to speed the searching process. "Command stacking," "nesting," and storing of search strategies are three examples of frequently-used techniques.

Command Stacking. Command stacking was mentioned briefly in Chapter 5; it refers to the ability to enter several commands at once. Commands must be separated from one another by a specified punctuation mark, such as the semicolon in DIALOG and SDC, and the forward slash (/) on BRS.

Nesting. Nesting allows the searcher to perform several Boolean operations at once. Most systems providing nesting utilize parentheses to make the search strategy explicit. For example, a search on "the effect of minimal brain damage on cognitive development and/or motor skills development" might be performed on BRS as illustrated in Figure 8.16.

Storing the Strategy. Once a workable search strategy has been developed, most systems offer the capability of storing the strategy for use with a different database or with a different file of the same database. Storing the search strategy across several files or databases is most helpful when free-text searching, because the controlled vocabulary terms differ by database. Strategies may also be stored for the production of monthly current awareness bibliographies or SDIs. An SDI search may be executed automatically by the system or explicitly executed each month by the searcher. The requirements for each system are listed in the manuals.

SUMMARY

This has been an overview of some of the search capabilities offered for online information retrieval. The list of capabilities presented here is by no means exhaustive. The searcher should become familiar with the documentation for the search systems and databases to identify the various options available. New capabilities are added frequently, and information about them usually appears in system or database newsletters or other publications.

```
BRS/PSYC/1967 - APR 1983

BRS - SEARCH MODE  - ENTER QUERY
    1_:    minimally-brain-damaged or minimal-brain-disorders
    RESULT      334

*   2_:    1 and (cognitive-development or motor-development)
    RESULT        4

    3_:   cognitive-development or motor-development
    RESULT      5176

*   4_:   1 and 3                          *(Three mechanisms of reaching
    RESULT        4                          the same goal.  Note use of
                                             nesting parentheses in
    5_:   cognitive-development              statements 2 and 7.)
    RESULT      4759

    6_:   motor-development
    RESULT      492

*   7_:   1 AND (5 OR 6)
    RESULT        4

    8_:   ..off
+CONNECT TIME  0:01:47 HH:MM:SS   0.030 DEC HRS    SESSION  1355+

EST PSYC COST:  C-HRS    DB-ROY  CIT-ROY  COMM    TOTAL
                $.48     $.45     $.00    $.21   $1.14
```

Figure 8.16 Psychological Abstracts on BRS.

The following exercises will provide practice in using the searching techniques presented in this chapter.

EXERCISES

Assume that each of these search requests was presented by a client. Search each request on any one of the three major search systems, DIALOG, SDC ORBIT, or BRS. Use the database(s) of your choice, unless otherwise instructed. Not all of these databases are available on every system. The databases may be found under different names on the systems which support them.

1. Locate any papers which cite published works by Lewis H. Kuller, a physician and epidemiologist.

2. What effect do the national trends which are disrupting "traditional" family life have on children's emotional development and/or performance in school? The specific trends of interest are these: divorce, frequent moving of households, and mothers employed outside the home. NOTE: Use the truncation capability in conducting your search.
3. Japanese businesses have achieved great success through the use of employee participation techniques, such as *quality circles*. What, if any, information is available which describes these techniques and/or their applicability to American industry?
   NOTE: In formulating your search, build a free-text search strategy which you can then "store" for use against appropriate files.
4. Using the Psychological Abstracts database, locate articles published since 1980 on the topic of depression in women. To insure relevant retrieval, limit the terms in your search to the title and descriptor fields.
5. Using any chemical dictionary file, identify the chemical formula for BCME (bischloromethyl ether), a potent carcinogen which was the subject of a book entitled *Building 6*.
6. Identify articles authored by Linus Pauling which appear in either Science Citation Index, Biological Abstracts, or Excerpta Medica.

9

Performance Measurement and Evaluation

Information retrieval systems are complex systems serving a variety of needs. At times it is necessary to evaluate how well the systems are serving those needs. This chapter explores several aspects of performance evaluation, beginning with some of the classical measures of system performance. Then searcher performance is discussed in terms of the searcher's ability to exploit the system capabilities. The last section discusses methods of evaluating client satisfaction with the system and the overall service.

Performance measurement and evaluation of information retrieval systems is a broad topic, with a large literature to support it. This chapter provides only a cursory overview of the issues most relevant to evaluating a searching service. The bibliography provides sources for further information on these issues.

SYSTEM PERFORMANCE

Classical Meaures

As information retrieval systems were developed, designers found it necessary to "benchmark" their performance. In order to improve a system, one needs a measure, or benchmark, of its current performance. These measures often are ratios based on quantities such as records retrieved from a database, relevant records in the database, relevant records retrieved, and total number of records in the database. The first set of such ratios was proposed by Kent, et al, in 1955 (1). They proposed six different measures which they called "factors": resolution, elimination, pertinency, noise, recall, and omission. A number of other measures have been proposed since, but only two remain in common use: precision (the "pertinency factor") and recall.

Precision is the ratio of relevant records retrieved to all records retrieved, expressed as the fraction

$$\frac{\textit{Relevant records retrieved}}{\text{All records retrieved}}$$

Recall is the ratio of relevant records retrieved to all the relevant records in the database, or the fraction

$$\frac{\textit{Relevant records retrieved}}{\text{Relevant records in database}}$$

Often these ratios are multiplied by 100 to express them as percentages. Note that the measures are based on individual searches rather than system performance as a whole.

Taken together, precision and recall measure the usefulness of the system output and the power of retrieval from the system. As with the other quantitative measures of system performance, they have some limitations which are discussed below.

Considerations in Applying the Classical Measures

Relationship of Precision and Recall Precision measures the efficiency with which the system achieves a particular recall ratio. For example, a search with 50% precision and 70% recall is more efficient than a search with 20% precision and 70% recall.

Precision also measures the amount of work that must be done after the search to sort out the relevant records.

Precision and recall tend to vary inversely. Increasing recall normally results in lower precision, since more irrelevant records are retrieved in the process of finding additional relevant records. Conversely, increasing precision tends to decrease recall.

Database Coverage Coverage is the proportion of all relevant literature contained in the database. (2) High recall on a low-coverage database is less valuable than high recall on a high-coverage database, for example. A client may judge recall in relation to the proportion of all literature on the topic retrieved, not in relation to what is in the particular database being searched.

Concept of Relevance The concept of relevance is the weakest aspect of the quantitative retrieval measures. All of the standard measures depend on relevance assessments, yet relevance itself cannot be measured precisely. Relevance is a personal judgement and therefore varies between individuals making the judgement. Further, the same individual may make different relevance judgements of the same records at different times. Some of the issues regarding the judgement of relevance include the following:

- Is the judgement of relevance based on a retrieved record the same as when the judgement is based on the full document?
- Is the relevance judgement of a searcher or experimenter the same as the relevance judgement of a motivated client?
- Does the order in which records are viewed influence the relevance judgement?
- Are records judged as relevant only in relation to the immediate search, or will a motivated client regard them as relevant because they are of general interest?

These questions and others remain unanswered, but it is important to note that any of these factors may influence the relevance judgement and hence the performance measures based on it.

Data Gathering Determining a precision measure for a search is straightforward: count the number of records retrieved and the number of them that are relevant, and divide. Determining the recall measure for a search is much more difficult, as it requires a count of all the relevant records in the database. In a small test database, it is possible to count all the relevant records for a specific search. In a large commercial database, this cannot be done.

Several methods have been developed for approximating recall measures, such as sampling techniques, assigning relevance to specific known records and then trying to retrieve them, and exhaustive searching of a topic to build a total recall set. For a discussion of these and other approaches, the reader is referred to Salton (3).

SEARCHING PERFORMANCE

Evaluating searching performance requires measuring both the searcher's ability to exploit the system and the searcher's ability to work with clients. While both are important, only the first topic is dealt with here; the other issues fall into the area of personnel management.

Classical Measures

The classical measures, such as precision and recall, can be applied to some aspects of searching performance. A searcher should understand the concepts of precision, recall, and relevance, and manipulate searches to achieve results within some desired range. Several of the more common applications of quantitative measures to search performance are discussed below.

Nature of the Search Request High precision or high recall does not necessarily imply a "good" search result; the measures must be appropriate for the client's needs. If a client seeks a comprehensive search for everything on a topic, he or she is requesting a high recall search. Clients with high recall needs will usually tolerate lower precision. They are willing to weed through more irrelevant retrieved documents in return for getting comprehensive coverage. A high recall search can be achieved by broadening the search, including more search terms, performing free text searching (where available), and sometimes by searching additional databases.

The client who seeks only "a few good references" has a high precision need. A high precision search can be achieved by narrowing the search, using fewer terms and those that are most likely to match. Some relevant items will be missed, but the proportion of irrelevant items will usually be decreased, as intended.

Searchers should not be judged purely on their ability to achieve high recall or high precision. Rather, they should be judged by whether the precision and recall measures were appropriate to the information request.

Standardized Searches A useful training and evaluation technique is to develop a standard set of searches with precision and recall measures for each, then have new searchers compare their performance to these standard measures. Developing such measures can be a cumbersome process, especially if estimating recall is required. A simple alternative is to use standardized searches developed by others. The DIALOG system, for example, supports several training databases called ONTAP (for "online training and practice"). Precision and recall measures have been established for specific searches on these files. A searcher can perform these searches and then compare the results with the optimal measures established.

Comparative Recall Another evaluation method is to compare a set of records retrieved on a search by an experienced searcher to the set of records retrieved by a new searcher or trainee. (4) To determine a comparative recall measure, the experienced searcher first performs a high recall search and records the records retrieved. The trainee then performs the same search and records the number of records retrieved (set "A"). Assuming that the experienced searcher found more records, the two sets are compared and the number of *additional* records found by the experienced searcher is recorded (set "B"). Comparative recall is the ratio A/(A + B). The larger the ratio is, the closer the trainee has come to achieving the recall of the experienced searcher.

Notice that the comparison is valid only for recall and not for precision. On a high precision search, two searchers might find sets of equal precision, but the content of the sets may have few, if any, records in common. In that case, neither search may be "better" than the other.

Analytical Procedures

Search performance can be analyzed by several criteria which are not necessarily quantitative, but are still useful. Several of these techniques are discussed below.

Search Failures As with any task, some searches will be more successful than others. Frequently, more can be learned from the failures than from the sucesses. Such an analysis begins with a variety of searches which are classified by degree of success or failure. The searches should be reviewed with the following questions in mind:

- Why did the failures occur?
- What distinguishes good searches from poor searches?
- Is the same search better when performed by one searcher than by another?
- Do searches in some subject areas get better results than those in other subject areas?
- Are searches with high recall or precision also better searches in other respects?

In performing the analysis, emphasis should be placed on identifying trends. These data can then be used to improve search techniques and produce output that is closer to the expressed needs of the clients.

Database Coverage As discussed earlier, search results must be evaluated with respect to the content of the database. Assessment of search performance should incorporate the choice of databases selected for the search. Recall may be artificially high in a low coverage database, for example, but this does not necessarily make it a good search.

Vocabulary Not only does database coverage vary, so does the use of vocabulary terms. Some database vocabularies use generic terms, others have specific indexing, and others have only free text. The searcher should consider the appropriateness of the database vocabulary for the search, as this too affects search success. Precision and recall measures are also affected by database vocabulary.

CLIENT SATISFACTION

Client satisfaction is perhaps the most difficult aspect to evaluate, since it is least under the searcher's control and is hard to quantify. In evaluating client satisfaction, the staff must first realize that satisfaction is largely a function of expectations. If a client receives as much or more than expected, he or she will probably be satisfied. Some of the expectations are based on information provided by the service about its capabilities; other expectations are outside the control of the service. For example, if a client has a generally positive or generally negative attitude toward the library or information center as a whole, it may carry over to the searching service no matter how competent the staff.

In evaluating client satisfaction, the performance of the search service is also being measured. Some of the critical points to evaluate are these:

- Did the clients receive output that met their recall/precision needs? That is, if they wanted a "few good references," is that what they received, or did they have to review (and pay for) many irrelevant records to get what they needed? If they wanted "everything on the topic," did it include everything that could be found in all the appropriate databases, or just a few good references?
- Did the clients receive their output in a timely manner? Or did it arrive too late to be of value?
- Did the clients feel that the searcher understood the search request and provided output accordingly?
- Did the clients have realistic expectations of the search outcome and were they satisfied?
- Were the clients satisfied with the service overall?

Such aspects of satisfaction can be evaluated either by formal methods such as surveys (Figure 9.1), or by informal methods such as discussions with the clients. These two approaches are discussed below.

Formal Evaluation Search services frequently survey their clients to evaluate satisfaction with the service and to determine additional improvements that may be needed. While surveys are useful, they should be performed with some discretion. Few clients will be pleased with filling out the same questionnaire after

STANFORD LIBRARIES
COMPUTER SEARCH SERVICE

1. Search No. ____
2. Library ____
3. Date ____

SEARCH EVALUATION

PLEASE TAKE A FEW MINUTES TO ANSWER THE FOLLOWING QUESTIONS TO HELP US IMPROVE THIS SERVICE AND TO HELP DETERMINE IF IT SHOULD BE CONTINUED. WHEN FINISHED, JUST FOLD AND STAPLE AND USE THE BACK OF THE FORM AS AN EVELOPE. RETURN IT TO:

____

THANK YOU

1. Was the information and assistance you received when you submitted the search adequate? ___ Yes ___ No
2. Was the time lapse between submitting and receiving your search reasonable? ___ Yes ___ No
3. Did the search produce the type of information you desired? ___ Yes ___ No
4. Compared with manual searching, did the computer search produce:
   ___MORE ___LESS ___ABOUT THE SAME amount of references?
5. Did the search results justify the expense? ___ Yes ___ No ___ Partly
6. Would you use the service in the future for similar problems? ___ Yes ___ No ___ Unsure
7. Where did you learn about the Computer Search Service? ___LIBRARIAN, ___POSTER, ___PRINTED ANNOUNCEMENT ___FRIEND/COLLEAGUE, ___OTHER ____
8. We welcome other comments about the service or about the bibliography you received.

Figure 9.1 Search evaluation form. (Used by permission of Stanford University Library.)

every search on a permanent basis. Instead, the service might be evaluated soon after if starts operation and again at regular intervals. Questions such as those listed above should be addressed in the questionnaire. For a review of questionnaires used by searching services, the reader is referred to Daniels (5).

Performing a formal survey is a more complex undertaking than it may appear on the surface. Some knowledge of survey construction, sampling techniques, and statistical analysis is required to perform a study properly. If not done well, a survey may provide erroneous results, which is worse than no results at all. Unless someone on the searching staff has a knowledge of research methods, it is recommended that appropriate consulting help be sought.

Informal Evaluation Well-established searching operations, particularly those which serve the same group of clients repeatedly, may find that informal evaluation methods are satisfactory. One such form of evaluation involves a discussion between the searcher and the client, both to review the output of a search and to identify any problems with the search or with any other aspect of the service. Good communication between the searching staff and the clients will help the staff remain sensitive to their needs and may provide information comparable to that provided by a formal study.

SUMMARY

Search services are complex operations and several of their aspects deserve evaluation. System performance can be evaluated using any of a number of quantitative measures, the most popular of which are precision and recall. When applying these measures, one must consider that they vary inversely, that they are dependent on database coverage, and that the measures are based on relevance, an ill-defined concept itself. Precision is easier to measure than is recall, since precision is based on retrieved output alone, whereas recall requires a knowledge of database content.

The quantitative measures applied to system performance are also useful in evaluating searching performance. Client needs can be classified into high-precision and high-recall searches. The searcher should be judged on ability to modify a search to meet these needs, rather than on precision or recall measures alone. These measures are also useful in training, when comparing the trainee's performance and recall measures with those achieved by experts.

Some analytical techniques for evaluating searching performance are also appropriate. Search results can be examined to determine the characteristics of failed searches, a process that includes an assessment of database selection by coverage and by vocabulary.

Client satisfaction is perhaps the most difficult to evaluate, as it cannot be quantified easily and is least under the control of the searcher. Client expectations are an important part of satisfaction. Such satisfaction can be evaluated either by formal or informal means. The use of formal evaluation methods, such as surveys, requires the application of appropriate research methods.

REFERENCES

1. Kent, A.; Berry, M. M.; Luehrs, F. U., Jr.; Perry, J. W. "Machine Literature Searching. VIII: Operational Criteria for Designing Information Retrieval Systems." *American Documentation*, Vol. VI, No. 2 (1955), p. 93-101.
2. Cleverdon, C. W. *Evaluation of Operational Information Retrieval Systems. Part 1: Identification of Criteria.* Cranfield, Eng.: College of Aeronautics, 1964.
3. Salton, G. *Automatic Information Organization and Retrieval.* New York: McGraw-Hill, 1968.
4. Lancaster, F. W.; Fayen, E. G. *Information Retrieval On-Line.* Los Angeles: Melville, 1973.
5. Daniels, L. "A Matter of Form." *ONLINE*, Vol. 2, No. 3 (1978), p. 31-39.

BIBLIOGRAPHY

Artandi, Susan. *An Introduction to Computers in Information Science.* 2nd ed. Metuchen, NJ: Scarecrow Press, 1972.

Bourne, Charles P., et al. *Requirements, Criteria, and Measures of Performance of Information Storage and Retrieval Systems.* Menlo Park, CA: Stanford Research Institute, 1961.

Cleverdon, Cyril W. "Design and Evaluation of Information Systems." In Cuadra, Carlos A.; Luke, Ann W., eds, *Annual Review of Information Science and Technology*, Vol. 6. Chicago: Encyclopedia Britannica, 1971.

Cleverdon, Cyril. "The Cranfield Tests on Index Language Devices." *Aslib Proceedings*, Vol. 19, No. 6 (1967), p. 173-194.

Cleverdon, Cyril W., et al. *Factors Determining the Performance of Indexing Systems*, Vol. 1 (Design), Vol. 2 (Test Results). Aslib – Cranfield Research Project. Cranfield, Eng.: Cranfield College of Aeronautics, 1966.

Cleverdon, Cyril W. *Evaluation of Operational Information Retrieval Systems. Part 1: Identification of Criteria.* Cranfield, Eng.: Cranfield College of Aeronautics, 1964.

Cuadra, C. A.; Katter, R. V. "Opening the Black Box of Relevance." *Journal of Documentation*, Vol. 23, No. 4 (1967), p. 291-303.

Daniels, Linda. "A Matter of Form." *ONLINE*, Vol. 2, No. 3 (1978), p. 31-39.

Doyle, Lauren B. *Information Retrieval and Processing.* Los Angeles: Melville Pub. Co., 1973.

Goffman, William. "On Relevance as a Measure." *Information Storage and Retrieval*, Vol. 2 (1966), p. 201-203.

Kent, Allen. *Information Analysis and Retrieval.* New York: Becker and Hayes, Inc., 1971.

Kent, A.; Berry, M.; Luehrs, F. U., Jr.; Perry, J. W. "Machine Literature Searching. VIII: Operational Criteria for Designing Information Retrieval Systems." *American Documentation*, Vol. VI, No. 2 (1955), p. 93-101.

Kent, A.; Taulbee, O. E.; Belzer, J.; Goldstein, G. D., eds. *Electronic Handling of Information: Testing and Evaluation.* Washington, DC: Thompson Book Co., 1967.

Kiewett, Eva L. *Evaluating Information Retrieval Systems: The Probe Program.* Westport, CT: Greenwood Press, 1979.

King, Donald W., ed. *Key Papers in the Design and Evaluation of Information Systems.* White Plains, NY: Knowledge Industry Publications, 1978.

Lancaster, F. W.; Fayen, E. G. *Information Retrieval On-Line.* Los Angeles: Melville Pub. Co., 1973.

Lancaster, F. Wilfrid; Gillespie, Constantine J. "Design and Evaluation of Information Systems." In Cuadra, Carlos A.; Luke, Ann W., eds. *Annual Review of Information Science and Technology*, Vol. 5. Chicago: Encyclopedia Britannica, 1970.

Lancaster, F. W. *Information Retrieval Systems: Characteristics, Testing, and Evaluation.* New York: Wiley, 1968.

Lancaster, F. W. *Evaluation of the MEDLARS Demand Search Service.* Washington, DC: National Library of Medicine, 1968. ED 022 494.

Lesk, M. E.; Salton, Gerard. "Relevance Assessments and Retrieval System Evaluation." *Information Storage and Retrieval,* Vol. 4, No. 3 (1968), p. 343-359.

Maron, M. E.; Kuhns, J. L. "On Relevance, Probabilistic Indexing and Information Retrieval." *Journal of the Association for Computing Machinery,* Vol. 7, No. 3 (1960), p. 216-244.

McGill, Michael; Koll, Matthew; Noreault, Terry. *An Evaluation of Factors Affecting Document Ranking by Information Retrieval Systems.* Syracuse, NY: School of Information Studies, Syracuse University, 1979.

Paisley, William J.; Parker, E. B. "Information Retrieval as a Receiver-Controlled Communication System." *Symposium on Education for Information Science.* Heilprin, Laurence B., et al, eds. Washington, DC: Spartan Books, 1965.

Perry, J. W.; Kent, Allen. *Documentation and Information Retrieval.* New York: Interscience, 1967.

Perry, J. W.; Kent, Allen; Berry, M. M. *Machine Literature Searching.* New York: Interscience, 1956.

Richmond, Phyllis A. "Review of the Cranfield Project." *American Documentation,* Vol. 14, No. 4 (1963), p. 307-311.

Salton, Gerard. *The SMART Retrieval System.* Englewood Cliffs, NJ: Prentice-Hall, 1971.

Salton, Gerard. "Evaluation Problems in Interactive Information Retrieval." *Information Storage and Retrieval,* Vol. 6, No. 1 (1970), p. 29-44.

Salton, Gerard. "Automatic Text Analysis." *Science,* Vol. 168, No. 3929 (1970), p. 335-343.

Salton, Gerard. *Automatic Information Organization and Retrieval.* New York: McGraw Hill, 1968.

Saracevic, Tefko. "The Concept of Relevance." In Saracevic, Tefko, ed., *Introduction to Information Science.* New York: R. R. Bowker, 1970.

Saracevic, Tefko. "Comparative Effects of Titles, Abstracts, and Full Texts on Relevance Judgements." *Proceedings of the American Society for Information Science*, 32nd Annual Meeting, Vol. 6. Washington, DC: ASIS, 1969, p. 293-299.

Swanson, D. R. "Searching Natural Language Text by Computer." *Science*, Vol. 132, No. 3434 (1960), p. 1099-1104.

Swanson, Rowena Weiss. "Design and Evaluation of Information Systems." In Cuadra, Carlos A.; Luke, Ann W.; Harris, Jessica L., eds., *Annual Review of Information Science and Technology*, Vol. 10. Washington, DC: American Society for Information Science, 1975.

Tessier, Judith A.; Crouch, Wayne W.; Atherton, Pauline. "New Measures of User Satisfaction with Computer-Based Literature Searches." *Special Libraries*, Vol. 68, No. 11 (1977), p. 383-389.

10

Equipment Considerations

Searching online information retrieval systems requires the use of computing equipment such as computer terminals and telecommunications connections to the computer. The organization supporting the search operation normally leases or purchases equipment for that purpose. A variety of types of equipment are available, and they serve diverse needs. Many requirements must be considered in selecting such equipment.

This chapter discusses the selection and preparation of a site for online searching, the types of telecommunications equipment and connections available, the types of terminals available, and the selection and use of the equipment.

SITE SELECTION

Planning Time

Selection of the site should occur early in the planning process, as it may take several weeks or months from the time the terminals and telephones are ordered to the time they are installed.

The Physical Site

The first step in establishing a searching operation is to select a site for housing the equipment and performing the searches. Several factors should be considered in this regard.

Accessibility The site should be as easily accessible by the clients of the service as is possible. A visible location may also stimulate interest and encourage use of the service.

Most libraries and other organizations providing online searching have only one service site in order to minimize equipment and other costs. In a large organization, however, centralizing services may create disadvantages for the clients. If multiple sites are affordable, decentralization may improve the service. Although this chapter addresses only single-site operations, organizations providing a wider range of services can easily adapt this information to their needs.

Privacy and Security An enclosed area provides privacy for conversations between the searcher and the client and reduces the noise problem caused by the printing equipment. Security for expensive equipment is also an important consideration.

Size of Searching Site The floor area in the site should be large enough to allow room for the equipment, the searcher, at least two clients, and some work space (a total of about 100 square feet). If the room can hold 6 to 10 persons at once, it can be used for demonstrationss as well.

Furnishings

The searching site should have a table for the terminal (unless it is a free standing model), chairs for the searcher and client(s), work space for search strategy development, and table or shelf space for manuals and search aids. If any search aids are in the form of microfiche, a microfiche reader must be available as well. Sufficient storage space for special forms, brochures, and paper supplies is also useful.

Electrical Requirements

The site must have adequate lighting and at least one three-pronged electrical outlet (to ensure a safety ground) for each terminal. An acoustic coupler may require a separate grounded receptacle as well; still another may be required for lighting. Outlets used for terminals and communications equipment should be on separate electrical circuits from any other equipment that uses power intermittently, such as electric typewriters and photocopying machines. To be safe, an independent circuit for the computer equipment is recommended.

Telecommunications Requirements

The searching site must have telephone lines for as many terminals as will be used simultaneously. If possible, an additional telephone would be helpful in making outgoing calls while the terminals are in use. It would also allow the searcher to call a "help line" at the site of the system or database without logging off the system. Telephone connections to computer terminals have special requirements which are discussed in the next section.

TELECOMMUNICATIONS

Searching commercially available information retrieval systems is usually performed at a location remote from the computer. The connection between a terminal and a computer is known as a "telecommunications" link (1). This link normally is accomplished by using available telephone lines and appropriate telecommunications equipment.

Equipment for Connecting the Terminal to the Computer

The terminal may be connected to the computer using any of three combinations of telephone equipment. Each combination has advantages and disadvantages.

Acoustic Coupler An Acoustic coupler is a device with two molded cups to hold the speaking and listening units of a telephone receiver, plus the ability to translate the computer signals into a form suitable for the terminal, and the terminal signals to a form suitable for the computer. To use a coupler, a telephone call is made to the computer or to a value-added (telecommunications) network or VAN (see Chapter 1). When the phone is answered with a special high-pitched tone, the handset is placed into the cups of the acoustic coupler (see figure 10.1 for an illustration).

A coupler has a modem (modulator/demodulator) built into it. A *modem* is a device which translates the digital signals of the terminal into analog signals for transmission over telephone lines, and translates analog signals received over telephone lines back into digital signals for use by the terminal.

The telephone used with a coupler for the terminal connection should be a direct outside line that does not go through a switchboard. Such a dedicated line minimizes possible breaks or interference in the telecommunications transmission.

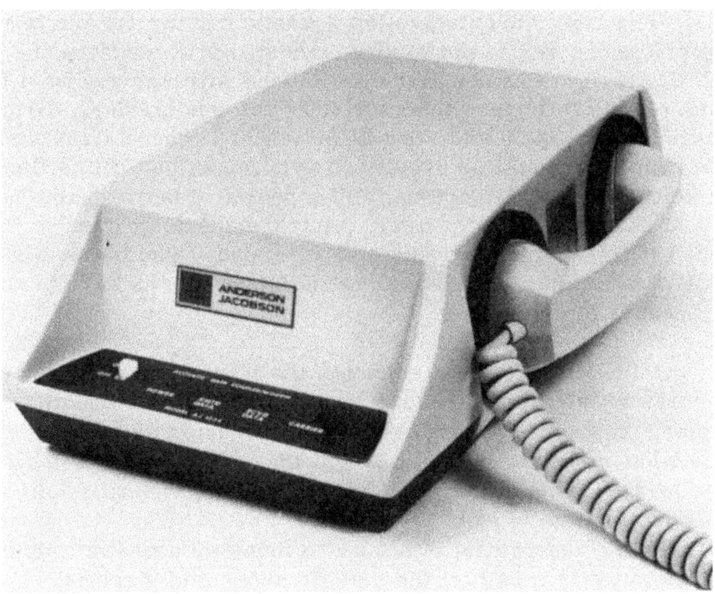

Figure 10.1 Acoustic coupler/modem. (Courtesy of Anderson Jacobson, Inc., San Jose, California.)

Figure 10.2 Portable terminal with built-in coupler in back. (Courtesy of Computer Devices Inc., Burlington, Massachusetts.)

The acoustic coupler may be a separate piece of equipment from the terminal, as in Figure 10.1. It is plugged into the terminal for the telecommunications connection and into a wall outlet for the power supply. Some terminals, particularly portable ones, have a coupler built into them (see Figure 10.2 for an illustration). The chief advantage of an acoustic coupler for the telecommunications link is portability. Independent couplers are small lightweight devices that can be used with any available telephone (although non-switchboard lines are preferable). Couplers installed in terminals add very little weight to the unit. Poorly made couplers should be avoided, however. A bad connection may introduce transmission errors, and a poor seal between the handset and the coupler might cause the telephone connection to be broken if the coupler is accidentally bumped. The better quality couplers maintain a connection that is as reliable as more permanent methods of connection.

Datasets A dataset connects the terminal directly to the computer or telecommunications network without the use of a coupler. It consists of a stationary telephone installed with a wall connection; between the dataset and the wall connection is a separate modem. The wall installation makes the terminal relatively permanent at that site.

Using the dataset is similar to using an acoustic coupler. The computer is called on the dataset phone and a special high-pitched tone is received. A button on the dataset is then pressed (or in some cases, pulled out) to lock in the connection. The dataset and modem can be leased or purchased from a commercial vendor. Figure 10.3 illustrates a dataset/modem combination.

Direct Modem Connection The third type of connection is made directly to a modem using a voice grade phone line. Such modems can be purchased or leased from the manufacturer. A permanent wall connection is necessary for the modem and it in turn is connected to the telephone without the use of an acoustic coupler. Figure 10.4 illustrates a standard modem.

Comparison of Connection Methods

The bumping problem is usually eliminated with the dataset or direct modem connections and the connection is more reliable than that of lower quality couplers. Datasets are more costly than couplers, but are more reliable in filtering out noise.

The choice between an acoustic coupler and the dataset and/or modem may be affected by the specific terminal used. This should be explored with the terminal equipment vendor as part of the selection decision. Another consideration is the speed of transmission (discussed in the next section). The connection equipment must operate at a speed less than or equal to that of the terminal. Some connection equipment (and terminals) can be switch-selected for different transmission speeds; others operate at only one speed.

Unless the terminal selected has specific connection requirements, the decision between an acoustic coupler and a dataset and/or modem is usually based on portability needs and cost. The dataset/modem connections are permanent, which means that the terminal can be used only where the equipment is installed. With an acoustic coupler, the terminal can be connected to any available telephone.

Signal Transmission over Telecommunication Lines

Transmission of signals for computing is done through a series of "bits." *Bit* is an abbreviation for "binary digit," meaning either 0 or 1. The entire alphabet, a set of numerals (0 through 9), and special characters (such as .,*#?) are represented by strings of 0's and 1's, or "bit strings." This is accomplished through a coding system in which strings of 7 or 8 bits represent each distinct character ("character," as used here, is a general term for letter, number, or special character). Two common coding

Figure 10.3 CRT terminal with dataset/modem combination. (Courtesy of Anderson Jacobson, Inc., San Jose, California.)

Figure 10.4 Modem. (Courtesy of Anderson Jacobson, Inc., San Jose, California.)

systems are used: ASCII (American Standard Code for Information Interchange) which is 7 bits plus a parity bit (8 bits total) for each character, and EBCDIC (Extended Binary Coded Decimal Interchange Code) which is 8 bits plus a parity bit. A parity bit is a nondata bit added to each set of character bits so that the total number of bits representing a character is either always odd or always even. Parity checking is a simple method of error detection.

Terminal Transmission Speeds

Most terminals operate at speeds ranging from 300 to 1200 bits per second, or roughly 30 to 120 characters per second (CPS). Higher speeds can be achieved with leased lines, but the receiving computers used for information retrieval systems normally do not provide communications for searching above 120 characters per second. Standard transmission speeds are 10, 15, 30, and 120 CPS, with 30 and 120 being the most common at this time. Some terminals can operate at only one speed, while most others can be switched to the desired speed. Transmission speeds can also be stated in terms of *baud rate* or bits per second (2). Baud rate is roughly ten times the rate for characters per second. For example, a speed of 300 baud is roughly the same as 30 CPS, and 1200 baud is approximately 120 CPS. The 10 to 1 ratio is due to the number of bits required to encode a single character. One character may be represented by a 7-bit ASCII code, plus a parity bit and start and stop bits, totalling 10 bits to transmit each character.

Searching at 1200 baud significantly increases the pace of interaction over searching at 300 baud, since information is displayed much more quickly. The increased pace is useful for viewing lists of index terms and references online. In addition, the decreased amount of connect time required for searching makes printing online less expensive, thus decreasing the need for offline printing. While 1200 baud increases the efficiency of experienced searchers, the pace may be disconcerting for those with less experience. It might be advisable for new searching operations to begin with 300 baud equipment and later upgrade to 1200 baud if desired. At present, 1200 baud equipment is significantly more expensive than is 300 baud, although it may be cost effective for high volume users. As 1200 baud equipment is increasingly used, the costs may come down to a point where the difference is no longer significant.

Compatibility of Data Encoding Systems

Most computers receive, store, and transmit data either in ASCII or EBCDIC code, but generally not in both. Communications between terminals and computers must be done in the same coding system or have translation programs change the transmission from one form to the other.

Most commercial information retrieval systems can accept transmissions in either ASCII or EBCDIC. It is in their marketing interest to accept transmissions from as wide a variety of terminals as possible. Computer systems serving a smaller range of users (such as the organization's internal system) may accept transmissions in only one code. If the terminal is to be used for other applications, the coding system for any other computers to be accessed should be identified before the terminal is selected. Thus a terminal can be chosen that will serve several purposes for the organization.

Telecommunications Mode

Telecommunications may be performed in half duplex or full duplex mode. The mode of transmission is independent of the speed of transmission. The mode determines whether transmissions can be flowing in both directions simultaneously or in only one direction. *Half duplex* mode allows transmission in only one direction (either to or from the computer) at a time. When the transmission is from the computer to the terminal, the terminal keyboard is "locked" until the transmission is completed. Once completed, the keyboard is released for keying the next transmission back to the computer.

Full duplex mode allows transmission in both directions simultaneously. If the searcher can anticipate the next command, it can be typed before the transmission from the computer is completed.

Half duplex is somewhat slower than full duplex, due to the waiting time. It does not have a significant impact on the total connect time, since much of the time online is spent keying, which is independent of mode or transmission speed.

Terminals and couplers are available as either full duplex only, half duplex only, or switch-selectable between full and half duplex. The coupler and terminal must be set to the proper transmission mode. Half duplex models are the least expensive; switch-selectable are the most common. They also come in *simplex* mode, which sends data in one direction only such as for a "receive only" printer.

Most of the commercially available systems can support transmissions in full duplex mode only; others can support both half and full duplex. Computers used for other purposes may be equipped for only one of the two modes.

Connecting the Terminal to the Computer

The two most common methods of making the link from terminal to computer are dial-up connections and leased lines.

Dial-up Connections Most searching on commercial retrieval systems is done by "dial-up" connections to the computer. A phone call – either local, long distance, or through a telecommunications network – is made to the desired computer. Dial-up connections make the use of the terminal flexible; any computer that has dial-up ports (and on which one is an authorized user) can be accessed by telephone. If a portable acoustic coupler is used, the connection can be made from any telephone to any computer by using the same terminal.

Leased Lines The alternative to a dial-up connection is a permanently connected leased line between the terminal and the computer. The line is leased from the telephone company, and the cost is too high to be justified by any but high volume, multiple-terminal users.

Once the terminal is connected to the leased line, it cannot be connected to another computer without first disconnecting it from the line, which can be done with a specially installed switch. Leased lines are used only when terminals will be connected to a computer for long periods of time, for example with cataloging databases such as OCLC Online Computer Library Center and the Research Libraries Information Network (RLIN). They would not be used for general purpose retrieval systems such as DIALOG, SDC, or BRS.

Leased lines have several advantages over dial-up connections. They can support higher transmission rates such as 4800 or 9600 baud, although they may be more susceptible to line interference problems since a minor perturbance may cause an error in a fast data flow. Many organizations prefer leased lines for security reasons; it is easier to keep unauthorized users out of the system with leased lines than with dial-up connections.

SELECTING A TERMINAL

Types of Terminals

Computer terminals can be grouped into two types: video terminals and printing or hard-copy terminals. A video terminal, commonly called a VDT (video display terminal) or a CRT (cathode ray tube) (3), displays data on a television-like screen. ("VDT" is the more general term now that video technologies other than CRTs are availabe.) A printing terminal is any type of terminal that produces output on paper by any of several printing methods, thereby producing "hard copy." Figures 10.5 and 10.6 illustrate these two types of terminals.

Video Display Terminals

Images can be displayed much faster on a video terminal than they can be printed on paper. To the user of a VDT, it may appear that individual lines of date "flash" onto the screen. Because the display is electronic, no noise is associated with it; therefore a VDT is very quiet compared to a printing terminal.

Figure 10.5 CRT terminal. (Courtesy of Perkin-Elmer, Terminals Division, Flanders, New Jersey.)

Figure 10.6 Printing terminal with numeric keypad. (Courtesy of General Electric, Data Communication Products Business Department, Waynesboro, Virginia.)

The amount of data that can appear on a VDT screen varies by individual terminal, but the standard size is 24 lines, each 72 to 80 characters in length.

Most VDTs can operate at 1200 baud (120 CPS) or faster and are less expensive than most printing terminals. They have fewer mechanical parts than do printing terminals, and tend to need less repair. For group demonstrations, video monitors can be connected to a video terminal, displaying multiple copies of the interaction to the audience. One VDT can drive several additional video monitors.

Printer/VDT Combinations

The chief disadvantage of a VDT is that no hard copy or permanent record of the interaction is made. The availability of a permanent record of at least certain portions of the interaction (such as citations displayed online) is needed for online searching. One solution to this problem is to use a printer in addition to the VDT, and print needed portions of the interaction selectively. This would mean less noise than printing the full interaction, but the acquisition of both a VDT and a printer increases the equipment costs. Relatively inexpensive "slave printers" could be used, which have no keyboard and print exactly what is on the screen. Higher quality printers with additional formatting and control features could also be used. One printer can be shared by several video display terminals.

While combining a VDT and a printer is perhaps the most practical approach, several technical problems should be considered. Terminals may need to be "buffered" (hold a certain amount of data) properly for the particular printer, and the printer must operate at a speed at least equal to that of the VDT. Other technical considerations may depend on the type of main computer. Equipment compatibility should be discussed with each equipment supplier prior to purchase.

Printing Terminals

Most printing terminals are physically similar to electric typewriters (see Figures 10.6, 10.7, 10.8, and 10.10). Their chief advantage is that a record of the entire transaction is generated. While a printing terminal typically costs more than a video display terminal, a single printing terminal may be less expensive than the combined cost of a VDT and a printer. The chief disadvantages of printing terminals are the noise they make while printing and their tendency to break down more often.

Figure 10.7 Printing terminal with numeric keypad. (Courtesy of Anderson Jacobson, Inc., San Jose, California.)

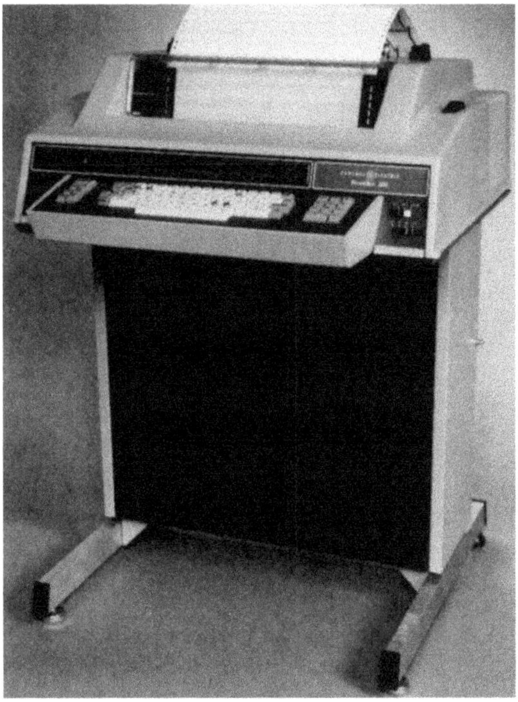

Figure 10.8 Stand-alone printing terminal with numeric keypad. Note switches on right to select full and half duplex modes and transmission speeds (10, 20, 30, and 120 characters per second). (Courtesy of General Electric, Data Communications Products Business Department, Waynesboro, Virginia.)

GENERAL CONSIDERATIONS IN SELECTING TERMINALS

Several general considerations apply to both VDT and printing terminals. These are discussed first, followed by specific considerations for selecting each type of terminal.

Size of Character Set

One of the first considerations in selecting a terminal is to ascertain whether it prints or displays characters in both upper and lower case or in upper case only. Some of the least expensive terminals are upper case only; however, displaying both upper

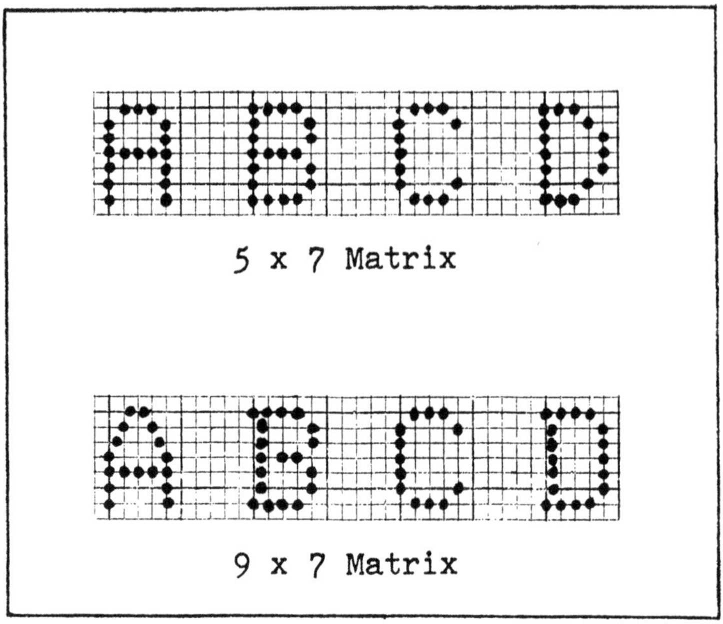

Figure 10.9 Dot Matrix Printing

and lower case letters is preferable for bibliographic searching. Print that is all upper case is harder to read and produces less attractive output. If the terminal is specified as "full 64-character ASCII," it is upper case only. It must be "full 96-character ASCII" to have upper and lower case capabilities.

Typeface

The quality of typefaces available on terminals varies enough to be an important consideration in the quality of output. Only impact printers, and of those only the slower ones, use a typeface which resembles that of an office typewriter. These are known as "letter quality printers" and are discussed below. Most of the high-speed impact printers, all non-impact printers, and VDTs, form characters through the use of the dot matrix technique.

A *dot matrix* is a grid of dots for forming individual characters. The least dense dot matrix is 5 x 7, or 5 dots across and 7 dots down. The most dense matrix normally available is 10 x 14,

Figure 10.10 Printing terminal used with a floppy disk drive. (Courtesy of Computer Devices Inc., Burlington, Massachusetts.)

with 5 x 7 and 9 x 7 matrices being the most common. A 5 x 7 matrix has a total of 35 dots with which to form a character, while the 10 x 14 matrix has a total of 140 dots. The denser the matrix, the easier the characters are to read (see Figure 10.9).

In evaluating the quality of dot matrix or other printers, examine the way the letters are formed. Some printers use small uppercase letters for lower case letters rather than the traditional method. Low density matrix printers (5 x 7 or 9 x 7) frequently do not descend tails ("descenders") of letters such as "y" and "g" below the line, making the print more difficult to read. The best print face for bibliographic searching is one which uses true lower case letters with descenders below the line.

Dumb vs. Smart Terminals

Terminals are often divided into two categories based on internal computing and storage capabilities: "dumb" and "smart" (also called "intelligent") terminals. This distinction is usually applied only to VDTs. Printing terminals are typically "dumb," although more "smart" printing terminals, particularly portable ones, have become available. The distinctions between dumb and smart terminals are not always clear; in some cases, additional options available on a dumb terminal may move it into the range of smart terminals. A clearer distinction can be made between those which are "teletype replacement" and those with more sophisticated capabilities (4). The "smartest" terminals are probably those which are computers themselves, such as the personal computers available with communications abilities.

Dumb Terminals Dumb terminals are the simplest and least expensive terminals available. They perform all the functions necessary for online searching. Dumb terminals may be the best choice for a searching operation with severe budget constraints or with a low volume of searching. Only if additional capabilities are needed should more expensive smart terminals be considered.

Smart Terminals Smart or intelligent terminals have built-in microcomputer capabilities and storage. These additions give the terminal some computing power, and support additional tasks such as submitting predefined searches and editing and sorting output. Smart terminals range from those with only a few more features than the dumb terminals to those sophisticated enough to be used as standalone microcomputers. Selection of smart terminals should be based on the inclusion of features that will actually be used, since there is a wide range in cost. While a terminal should not be rejected because it has additional options, there is no point in paying for unused features.

Offline Uses of Smart Terminals A smart video display terminal can be used "offline" (not connected to the computer) both for entering and manipulating data. Data entered into the terminal when it is offline can be transmitted directly to the computer at a later time when the terminal is connected online. The terminal and the computer interact at high speeds without the time lag necessary for keying the data online. Data such as references can be sent from the information retrieval system to the terminal for processing, and transferred later from the terminal to a printer. Connect time can thus be significantly reduced through offline use of smart terminals.

Smart terminals can also be connected to separate offline storage devices such as cassettes or floppy disks (5). Data is keyed into the terminal and loaded from the terminal to the cassette or floppy disk, or data from an online search is transferred directly from the terminal (while online) to the separate storage medium. Figures 10.10, 10.11, and 10.12 illustrate terminals connected to separate storage devices.

Using Offline Capabilities for Input Offline capabilities can be used to store the logon procedures in the terminal and build search strategies. These data are stored in the terminal, the computer is dialed up and the connection made, and the logon protocol and search strategy are submitted directly. If the strategy requires refinement, the searcher can either alter it online or logoff, refine the strategy in the terminal, log back on, and resubmit the strategy (6, 7).

Data created offline can be stored on a cassette or floppy disk as well as in the terminal. This approach is particularly

Figure 10.11 Portable computer with printer, cassette drive, two floppy disk drives, and a dataset. (Courtesy of Computer Devices Inc., Burlington, Massachusetts.)

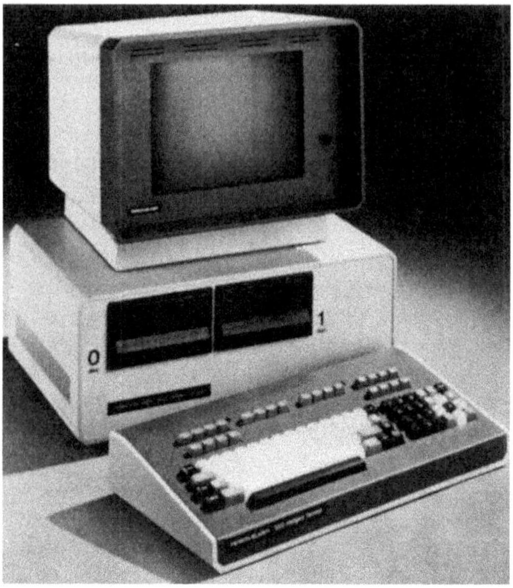

Figure 10.12 CRT terminal with detachable keyboard, used with dual floppy disk drive. (Courtesy of Perkin-Elmer, Terminals Division, Flanders, New Jersey.)

useful for SDI searches. The searches can be recorded on the cassette or floppy disk offline or while first being performed online, and then resubmitted periodically. Storing searches has the additional advantage that the data is saved if the computer goes down or if any other interruption occurs during the online search.

Using Offline Capabilities for Output The storage and computing capabilities of smart terminals are useful for manipulating the output of searching. Rather than selecting relevant references online or printing output which may contain non-relevant items offline, all online search output can be stored, either in the terminal or on another storage medium. The computing capabilities of the terminal can sort and edit the output, and the client could even review the output on the VDT and make relevance judgements before the final printing is done.

Smart terminals with these capabilities, or the addition of external storage devices, are much more expensive than a minimal equipment configuration. However, costs are dropping as their use increases. Such equipment minimizes search costs, and the search system vendors are aware of this. The original charging computations were designed for 150 to 300 baud searching, with all keying done online and most printing done offline at the search system site. As more use is made of sophisticated equipment, search system charges are changing accordingly. Some systems have already begun to charge for online record display.

CONSIDERATIONS IN SELECTING VIDEO DISPLAY TERMINALS

Several additional considerations should be explored in selecting a video display terminal to ensure that it is appropriate for database searching and contains the best capabilities for the cost (8). Video display terminals are illustrated in Figures 10.3, 10.5, 10.12, 10.13, and 10.14. These are only a sampling of the wide variety of VDTs available.

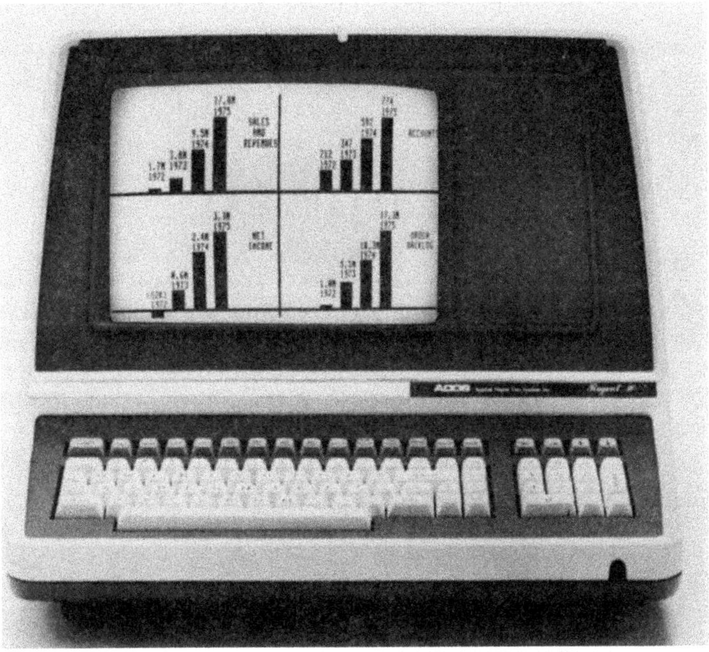

Figure 10.13 CRT terminal with graphics capabilities, editing, and function keys, and numeric keypad. (Courtesy of Applied Digital Data Systems Inc., Hauppauge, New York.)

Figure 10.14 CRT terminal with detachable keyboard, numeric keypad, variable size print display, and reverse video capabilities. (Courtesy of Digital Equipment Corporation, Maynard, Massachusetts.)

Screen Size

Among the first criteria for selecting a VDT is screen size. Many less expensive VDTs have screens that are too small for the standard displays of bibliographic data. The most legible terminals are those having at least 24 lines of display and a line width of 72 to 80 characters. One problem with using personal computers as searching terminals is that most of them have a much smaller screen display.

Connections to Other Devices

If the video display terminal is to be used with a printer, the VDT must have an external device interface. This is a standard feature but may not be available on the least expensive terminals. A smart terminal that is to be used with separate storage media such as cassettes or floppy disks must have connections for those devices as well. In most cases the external device connection is referred to as an "RS232 interface."

Clarity of Screen Display

Another consideration in selecting a VDT is the clarity of the screen display. Characters should be crisp and distinctly defined; they should not waver, and should be the same size at all points on the screen.

Editing Capabilities

Some VDTs, particularly smart ones, have editing keys. The simplest editing keys, sometimes available on dumb terminals, are insertion and deletion keys. These allow additional characters to be added or removed within a line while the rest of the line opens up or closes without being retyped. More sophisticated editing features include function keys that will duplicate or clear parts of a line, tab controls, and various composition features. Such capabilities simplify error corrections, particularly for poor typists, and may thus reduce connect time.

Scrolling Feature

Smart video terminals may also have a feature known as "scrolling." Rather than blanking out the whole screen when it becomes full of data, and starting the next line at the top, the new line is added at the bottom of the screen and the top line is scrolled off. This capability allows lines scrolled off the top of the screen to be scrolled back on command and redisplayed. Scrolling requires an internal memory ("buffer") in the terminal for storing the scrolled data.

CONSIDERATIONS IN SELECTING PRINTING TERMINALS OR PRINTERS

Printing devices include both printing terminals and separate printers for video display terminals. Printing terminals have a keyboard and are used in lieu of a VDT. Printers for VDTs generally do not have keyboards, although keyboard terminals may be connected to a VDT as a printer. Figures 10.15 and 10.16 illustrate non-keyboard printers. The criteria for selecting printing terminals and printers are about the same, so they are discussed together.

Figure 10.15 Free-standing printer. (Courtesy of General Electric, Data Communications Products Business Department, Waynesboro, Virginia.)

Types of Printing Mechanisms

Printing devices can be divided into two categories based on the printing mechanism. *Impact printers* generate characters by having a typeface strike or "impact" the paper. *Non-impact printers* do not strike the paper with a typeface; instead, the image is created by chemical, thermal, or electromagnetic means. The small printers suitable for online searching (both impact and non-impact) range in speed from 10 to 165 characters per second (CPS). Printing terminals are available in the same speeds as slower VDT transmission (10, 15, 30, and 120 CPS).

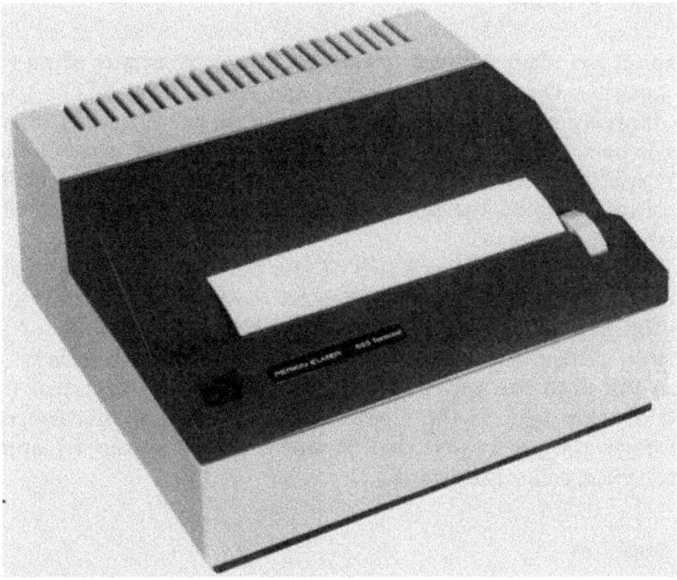

Figure 10.16 Simple table-top printer. (Courtesy of Perkin-Elmer, Terminals Division, Flanders, New Jersey.)

Impact Printers

Impact printing devices actually strike the paper surface with the type font and are thus the only kind that can be used with multi-part paper to make multiple copies. They are the noisiest of the devices due to the sound of the typing element striking the platen. Because they are primarily mechanical machines (as opposed to electronic, such as VDTs), impact printers have more moving parts to wear out and generally have higher maintenance costs.

Some of the slower impact printers use a type font similar to a typewriter. Known as "letter quality" printers, they produce the most attractive printed output. Some letter quality printers use an interchangeable IBM Selectric "golf ball" typing element. Others use a "daisy wheel" printing element that is also interchangeable, although it is more fragile. Interchangeable typing elements with multiple typefaces provide more flexibility in the use of the equipment. Most letter quality printers print at speeds up to 30 CPS.

Non-Impact Printers

Non-impact printing devices create an image by means of an interaction between the printing element and the surface of the paper, rather than by striking the paper. Because of this interaction, all non-impact printers are dot matrix printers and most of them require specially treated paper. They also cannot create multiple copies since to do so the printing element must have direct contact with the paper.

Perhaps the most popular of the non-impact printers is the thermal printer, which operates by moving a heated stylus across the paper, essentially "burning" the image onto it. Another type of non-impact printer uses an ink jet that sprays charged ink onto the paper in patterns formed by electrical fields. A third common type is the electrostatic printer, which electrically charges the paper and then moves a stylus across it, applying a toner to raise the image.

Paper Supplies

Each type of non-impact printer requires a special, unique, and expensive kind of paper. Adequate supplies must be kept on hand since it is not an item that is readily found in retail stores, nor can it be replaced by standard office paper. The special paper can be purchased through the terminal supplier or some other equipment or office specialty supplier. It tends to decay more rapidly than standard paper, particularly thermal paper which develops a gray cast. Electrostatic paper has a silver foil surface and prints with a black dot matrix. It can be somewhat difficult to read, but it photocopies quite well. Photocopying the printed output is a good method of checking for print clarity and assessing its usefulness for wider distribution.

Comparison of Impact and Non-Impact Printers

Non-impact printers are the fastest of the printing devices for bibliographic searching. Many of these operate in the 120 to 150 CPS range. They are typically less costly than impact printers, although there are expensive non-impact printers and inexpensive impact printers. Their print is less easy to read than that of letter quality printers, but the finer the matrix the better the quality of print. Non-impact printers are much quieter than impact printers, and are usually more reliable since they have fewer moving parts that require maintenance.

OTHER CONSIDERATIONS IN EQUIPMENT PURCHASE DECISIONS

Portability

Portable terminals provide a great amount of flexibility in a searching operation. Demonstrations to groups of current or potential clients can be made in places other than the searching site, and searches can be performed from the client's office, the searcher's home or second office, or from distant places while traveling. Many portable terminals weigh less than 20 pounds (including a built-in coupler) and have a carrying case or handle, and will fit easily under an airline seat. In a multiple-terminal searching environment, at least one portable terminal is probably needed.

Virtually all portable terminals are printing terminals. Recent VDT technology has advanced enough to provide portable display terminals, although most are thermal, dot matrix printers. Until recently, almost all portable terminals operated at 300 baud, which was a constraint for those who prefer 1200 baud searching. Portable 1200 baud terminals are now available. Smart portable terminals that have enough storage to allow searches in advance are also available.

If only one terminal is to be acquired for the searching operation, and remote use is not anticipated, a portable terminal may not be an appropriate choice. If the searching site is not well secured, a heavy, non-portable terminal may be preferred because it is less susceptible to theft.

Lease or Purchase of Equipment

Computer terminals, printers, and acoustic couplers can be leased on a contract basis or purchased outright. The decision to lease or purchase may be a matter of organizational policy and the searching staff may not have the choice.

If a lease/purchase decision is to be made, several factors should be taken into consideration. For a new searching operation, particularly with relatively inexperienced searchers, it may be wise to lease the equipment initially. When the operation is well established, the staff may have a better idea of exactly what equipment is most appropriate for permanent use.

Computing equipment is a high technology industry, and new products are continually being offered and pricing structures changed. If a piece of equipment is likely to become obsolete soon, purchase should be avoided. When a particular model is discontinued, obtaining service may be difficult.

Equipment Maintenance

Availability of maintenance is one of the most crucial considerations in selecting equipment. No matter how superb the piece of equipment, if it cannot be readily repaired it is not a good choice. A nonfunctioning terminal is of little value to any operation.

Maintenance services are available from the equipment manufacturer, the leasing company or terminal broker, or from a third party leasing firm. Service by the manufacturer is usually preferable. Large manufacturers service most areas, while smaller companies may provide service only in areas where they have enough installed equipment to justify the cost. Satisfactory service may be available from the broker or service firm as well.

Typically three types of arrangements can be made for maintenance: contract, time and materials, or depot maintenance. Maintenance on contract requires a monthly fee for each piece of equipment to be maintained. Having the highest priority of service for the maintenance organization, it guarantees service in a specified amount of time and fixes the maintenance cost in advance. Time and materials arrangements have no regular monthly payments, but require payment of an hourly rate for labor, plus parts and travel. Being of lower priority than maintenance contracts, repairs are not made as quickly. If the repairs are major, the bill could be very high. Depot maintenance requires the equipment to be carried or shipped to a repair point, where it will be returned when repairs are completed. Labor, parts, and shipping are charged for the service. Unless the searching operation has a surplus of terminals, the delays of depot maintenance are intolerable. For most organizations, a maintenance contract is the most feasible method of equipment support.

SUMMARY

Online searching requires computing equipment that is normally located at a dedicated search site. The responsibility for selecting a site usually falls on the searching staff, as may the responsibility for selecting the equipment.

The searching site should be selected and prepared in conjunction with the equipment decision. It should be large enough to accommodate the searcher, the client, the equipment, and furnishings, and it should be both convenient and private.

The next step is to select the equipment and establish the telecommunications requirements. These decisions include the choice between a VDT, a printing terminal, or a VDT in combination with a printer. Choices also must be made between dumb or smart terminals, impact or non-impact printers, and between matrix or letter-quality print.

Telecommunications needs will be based on the types of terminal and printing equipment selected, portability requirements, and the systems to be accessed. These needs must be determined before final decisions can be made on acoustic couplers, datasets, and/or modems; half or full duplex equipment; transmission speed and coding system; and use of direct dial, value-added networks, or leased lines.

Other decisions include whether to lease or purchase the equipment, and the most suitable type of maintenance contract.

REFERENCES AND NOTES

1. *Telecommunications*: (a) Pertaining to the transmission of signals over long distances, such as by telegraph, radio, or television (b) Data transmission between a computing system and remotely located devices via a unit that performs the necessary format conversion and controls the rate of transmission. (*Glossary of Computer Terms* (Revised). Kansas City, MO: DataPhase Systems, 1979.)
2. *Baud*: a unit of signaling speed equal to the number of discrete conditions or signal events per second. For example, one baud equals one bit per second in a train of binary signals. (*Glossary of Computer Terms, op. cit.*)
3. *Cathode Ray Tube*: An electronic vacuum tube, such as a television picture tube, that can be used to display graphic images in visual display terminals. Abbreviated CRT. (*Glossary of Computer Terms, op. cit.*)
4. Bonn, Jane H. and Heer, Phillipp R. "Terminal Equipment for On-Line Interactive Information Retrieval using Telecommunications." Special Libraries, Vol. 67, No. 1 (1976), p. 30-35.
5. *Cassettes* and *cassette tapes* are the same type of storage used in home stereo systems. A tape recorder/player both records and reads data to and from the cassettes.

A *floppy disk* (sometimes known as a "diskette") is a magnetic storage device in which the storage medium is a single flexible plate of Mylar material housed in a paper jacket, similar to a small record album. A disk drive records data onto the disk and reads it back.

6. Christian, Roger W. *The Electronic Library: Bibliographic Data Bases, 1978-1979.* White Plains, NY: Knowledge Industry Publications, 1978.
7. Steffenson, Martin B. and King, Kathryn. "Prerecord Your Online Bibliographic Searches for Time and Money Savings." *ONLINE*, Vol. 5, No. 1 (1981), p. 47-49.
8. For a discussion of terminal selection for online searching, see: Crawford, Walt. "CRT Terminal Checklist." *Journal of Library Automation*, Vol. 13, No. 1 (1980), p. 36-44.

BIBLIOGRAPHY

Bonn, Jane H. and Heer, Phillipp R. "Terminal Equipment for On-Line Interactive Information Retrieval Using Telecommunications." *Special Libraries*, Vol. 67, No. 1 (1976), p. 30.

Christian, Roger W. *The Electronic Library: Bibliographic Data Bases, 1978-1979.* White Plains, NY: Knowledge Industry Publications, 1978.

Crawford, Walt. "CRT Terminal Checklist." *Journal of Library Automation*, Vol. 13, No. 1 (1980), p. 36-44.

ONLINE Terminal Guide Directory, 1979-1980. Weston, CT: Online, Inc., 1978.

Steffenson, Martin B. and King, Kathryn. "Prerecord Your Online Bibliographic Searches for Time and Money Savings." *ONLINE*, Vol. 5, No. 1 (1981), p. 47-49.

11

Sources of Training

Gaining access to a commercial online information retrieval system is relatively simple. All that is needed is a terminal, an acoustic coupler, a telephone, and a password. However, for these systems to be of any practical value they must be searched effectively. Online information retrieval systems are basically a computerized method of searching the same literature and data available in a manual environment, but with many new capabilities. In many ways they are more difficult to search than manual indexes because of their flexibility and the inability to browse through literature. Using online systems poses some unique pressures, such as the pace of interaction with the computer and being aware of direct and indirect costs.

People who will be searching online systems, either for their own use or as search intermediaries to provide information to a client, need to be adequately trained both in the use of the software system and in the specifics of the particular database. As the number of available databases and online systems grows, the importance of searcher training increases.

Training pays for itself in several ways. First, a well-trained searcher is a better searcher and provides a better product to the client. Second is the ability to perform more cost-effective searches. This reduces costs for both the organization and the client. Third is the professional satisfaction that comes from a job well done (1).

This chapter provides a survey of training available in the use of online information retrieval systems, covering both formal and informal sources of training. Formal sources of training include those available from search service vendors, database suppliers, library schools, library and information networks, professional organizations and user groups, and other organizations. Informal sources include professional and journal literature, textbooks, and various reference materials. Computer-assisted forms of instruction are discussed separately, since they are available in either a formal or an informal context. This chapter is by no means an exhaustive list of the types of training courses and materials available. It is intended as an overview to make the reader aware of the resources that may be utilized for improving current skills and for maintaining skills over the course of a professional career.

WHAT TYPE OF TRAINING IS NEEDED?

Knowledge and Skills Required

Two general classes of knowledge and skills need to be learned. The first is system-independent skills, or general principles of searching. These include concepts of information retrieval, the reference interview for online searching, problem analysis, planning and search strategy development, Boolean logic, and the use of terminals and telecommunication equipment. Such basic information has been the focus of this text.

The second class of skills is system-dependent, or what must be learned about the particular search systems that are used. These skills include logging on to the system and logging off, the use of commands or protocol, entry formats for search terms, the implementation of Boolean logic, and database design. All searchers need exposure to general principles of searching, mechanics of one or more search systems, search strategy development, and evaluation of the results of searches. They also need to know the structure and contents of the databases they will be using, and something about how those databases will be handled online with different search systems. As searchers become more experienced, they need to learn more sophisticated techniques of searching and evaluation, and the specifics of more databases. Search systems continually improve and new capabilities are added; databases change in scope and policy and new databases are created. Searchers need to stay current with these changes.

The Learning Process

The learning process can be divided into four general stages as searchers gain increasing skills. The first stage is learning *what* is to be learned. The searching student begins by gaining a general understanding of what search systems are and just what knowledge and skills must be acquired. This stage is followed by learning the basic mechanics and procedures of searching. For some searchers, this second stage may be completed in a one or two day workshop; for others it may take weeks or months.

The third stage is the process of integrating search skills and knowledge to the point that the searcher is comfortable and fluid in searching procedures, a process that frequently takes several months. The last stage is the development of searching skills to a fully professional level. Skills are "fine-tuned," and the searcher becomes more efficient, more cost effective, and more comfortable with searching. This last stage includes keeping up with new systems and databases as well as changes in existing ones.

The amount of training and search experience required to progress through these stages varies greatly with each individual. Some searchers require a minimal amount of formal training, and learn additional skills easily and quickly from informal sources. Others need considerable formal training over a prolonged period of time. A wide spectrum of training resources are presented in this chapter to aid the searcher in selecting those resources needed for personal skill development.

Not all searchers are trained through formal mechanisms. One study found that only 55 percent of all searchers were formally trained by search system or database suppliers (2). Most of the rest were informally trained in some way, such as receiving on-the-job training from others who were trained by search service vendors or by self study of user manuals. Many of those learning to search online systems may at some time in their career have the responsibility of training others in search techniques.

TRAINING BY ONLINE SEARCH SERVICE SUPPLIERS

Online search service suppliers were the first to offer training to searchers on a large scale, and they have made a significant contribution to the training of searchers. Their staff are specifically responsible for training activities in system usage and in certain databases. Search service vendors produce many training and reference materials as well.

Training by Major Search Service Vendors

The three major multi-database search service vendors (DIALOG, SDC, and BRS) all provide similar types of training services. The first level of training consists of introductory seminars or workshops, intended as the first introduction to online searching. They cover general principles of searching, the use of terminals and dial-up procedures, search strategy construction, system command language, and an introduction to commonly used databases. They normally provide hands-on training, and sometimes offer additional online practice time at the searcher's site, either included in the cost of the session or at a reduced rate.

The next level of training is a refresher or update session. This type of session is a review of new features recently added to the system (or soon to be added), and new or changed databases. Update sessions may also include some advanced training, such as cost-effective search techniques.

The third level is the advanced searching workshop or seminar, which concentrates on the more sophisticated features of the search system and may be tailored to the specific group being taught. Such training may overlap with the intermediate level of instruction by providing information on new services and databases offered.

The highest level of training offered by the search service vendors are database-specific sessions, which may cover one or several related databases. These sessions provide detailed information on the content and coverage of the individual databases, and training in their effective use. Comparisons among databases in the same subject area are sometimes made. Some of the database-specific training sessions are sponsored jointly by the search service vendor and the database vendor, with representatives of both organizations available at the session.

Training sessions at all levels are generally available at the search service vendor's site, at regional sites, or at the customer site. They are frequently organized in conjunction with conferences held by organizations whose members have some interest in online searching. New user sessions are generally one to two days in length, while advanced user sessions may only be a half day. They are often customized to the needs of the group being trained (3).

In addition to formal training, all three major online services have toll-free telephone numbers, answered by experienced searchers, to assist with specific questions. Questions that come in on these "help lines" are often published later in "search hints" sections of the vendor newsletters.

Training by Other Search Service Vendors

The National Library of Medicine (NLM) was the first search service vendor to offer extensive training for its own services. They originally held an eight month training program for the batch-oriented Medical Literature Analysis and Retrieval System (MEDLARS). Later they offered a three week course for its online MEDLINE system, eventually replacing that with a five-level series of instruction. The NLM program remains one of the most extensive training programs offered (4).

Other online service vendors such as The Information Bank and BASIS also offer training on their respective systems. Training for some of the smaller services is sometimes included in the start-up contract with no additional fees required. In other cases, additional fees may be charged for various levels of training and for training materials.

TRAINING BY DATABASE PRODUCERS

Training programs offered by search service vendors are aimed at teaching the skills required to operate their particular system with a number of different databases. The training programs offered by database producers focus on a single database and are far less generalized in the range of instruction. This type of instruction covers the aspects of a database that a searcher must know to search it effectively: content coverage, criteria for inclusion of records in the database, indexing policies, other editorial policies, and search strategy construction. Once a searcher has become proficient in the use of a search system, training by a database producer can be an effective method of developing skills on databases that will be used regularly.

Frequently, the same database is available on more than one search system and there are differences in the way it is searched on each. Database producers may either structure the training independent of the search system or demonstrate use of the database on each system through which it is available. Searchers generally prefer the latter approach, but agreement is not universal.

Instruction by database producers tends to be similar to that offered by search system vendors, with workshops, continuing education programs, and reference aids. However, there are differences in the depth of training offered by individual producers. Some programs contain several levels of training (new, intermediate, advanced), while others offer only introductory sessions. Some produce a single reference aid, while others provide extensive manuals and thesauri. Some of the suppliers charge fees of several hundred dollars for their training sessions; others provide training free of charge (5). Like vendors, database producers may provide "help" lines to answer specific search questions and may also publish newsletters that include search hints.

TRAINING OFFERED BY SCHOOLS OF LIBRARY AND INFORMATION SCIENCE

Searching online information retrieval systems is an applied technology. As with other applied technologies, it was necessary to train in the field until the technology was well established. Schools of library and information science are now offering formal courses of instruction in searching bibliographic retrieval systems.

The library school courses provide basic instruction in the use of search systems and are not intended to produce fully trained searchers. Some courses are taught by library school faculty and others are taught by trained searchers from the university libraries or outside organizations. In some library schools, search system instruction is incorporated into introductory courses in reference, cataloging, library automation, or information science. In other schools, a complete course in searching online systems is offered. A few schools have developed laboratory training facilities that serve the community as well as the school. These are discussed later in this chapter.

TRAINING OFFERED BY OTHER ORGANIZATIONS

Other organizations offering training range from user groups to library networks to private consulting firms. Some groups offer complete training, while others serve as sponsors to set up local training sessions by vendors or other training groups.

Networks

Some of the library networks and consortia offer training, and some networks will also perform searches for libraries that do not have their own searching operations. Others will act as a unit to obtain group rates for member libraries.

One network offering online training is EDUNET. Organized by EDUCOM, it is a national computer network established to support computer-based resource exchange among colleges, universities, and research organizations throughout the United States. EDUNET currently makes available both the TRAINER and WISE systems. TRAINER is a computer-assisted instruction package developed by the University of Pittsburgh, which may be accessed on the Carnegie Mellon University computer (6). The WISE system, located at the University of Wisconsin, is a bibliographic search system supporting the ERIC databases.

Online User Groups

Many online user groups have been formed throughout the United States. These groups are usually organized by searchers in a geographic region for the purpose of sharing information. New searchers are sometimes paired with more experienced searchers so that they have a person to call for assistance. User groups may have newsletters that carry announcements of upcoming training sessions offered by system and database vendors, schedules of local meetings, columns on searching tips, general announcements, and a variety of other information. Some groups also publish searching aids and membership directories.

Most user groups hold regular meetings with specialized topics, discussion groups, and guest speakers. They are especially helpful for organizing locally-held training sessions, which usually require a minimum attendance. These groups can be identified through other searchers, through professional organizations, and articles and columns in professional literature. For example, ONLINE regularly publishes a user group directory.

Training Support Offered by Professional Organizations

Professional organizations in the areas of library and information science are useful sources of continuing education in online searching. Each of the three major professional organizations – the American Library Association, the American Society for Information Science, and the Special Libraries Association– have at least one, if not several, special interest groups related to searching online retrieval systems. More specialized organizations, such as Medical Libraries Association and American Association of Law Libraries also have groups interested in online searching.

These special interest groups hold topical sessions at annual and regional meetings of the parent organization, and may hold separate meetings as well. Most of these meetings are oriented toward issues and updating rather than training sessions in individual search systems or databases. Some may include demonstrations of systems, however, particularly those systems that are new or recently updated.

Private Sources of Training

As more searchers leave libraries to form private firms supplying information services, there will be more sources of training in the private sector. Some consulting groups already offer introductory training as well as training in specialized areas such as numeric databases. Announcements of training sessions may be listed in user group calendars, but many are also advertised by direct mail, using mailing lists obtained from related professional organizations and journal publishers.

COMPUTER-ASSISTED SOURCES OF TRAINING

Computer-assisted training is currently used primarily in universities and experimental programs. It has generally proven successful, with the major constraint being cost.

Computer-assisted training is discussed separately from other forms of training since it differs considerably from standard classroom and hands-on training. For the purposes of this discussion, it includes computer-assisted instruction (CAI), emulators, and other types of computer-supported training.

Computer-Assisted Instruction (CAI)

Computer-assisted instruction utilizes computer programs to teach and test in an interactive mode. CAI systems may be any combination of emulation of a system, sets of written instructions, quizzes or tests, "help" messages to augment regular instructions, and so forth. This technique is very useful for teaching online searching since the instruction is performed in the same interactive mode as actual searching. CAI also helps new users overcome any anxiety related to computing equipment – it combines the medium and the message of interactive searching.

Computer-assisted instruction allows the student to work at his or her own pace and to review previous lessons. When a message is unclear, most CAI systems allow the student to type a "help" request and receive further instructions. CAI systems generally do not require connection to the full search system, so connect time costs are far less than that of actual interactive searching. This allows the student to have much more online practice than would be cost-feasible on the full search system (7, 8, 9).

The National Library of Medicine has been using a CAI system, MEDLEARN, as part of its MEDLINE instructional package since 1973. (10) MEDLEARN teaches MEDLINE in an online, interactive mode, and is the required first level of instruction in MEDLINE training.

Search System Emulators

System emulators are software systems built to copy or emulate another system. Emulators have been designed to look like a specific search system, such as DIALOG. The protocol used to search the system is identical, and the functioning appears to be identical. The major difference is that the emulator operates on a local computer and searches small subsets of databases.

One emulator system that has been quite successful supports the University of Pittsburgh's "On-Line Bibliographic and Information Systems: A Training Center for Librarians and

Information Specialists," also known as the Online Training Center (not the same as the TRAINER system). The University has built search system emulators for each of the three major systems (DIALOG, SDC ORBIT, and BRS) (11). The emulators reside on a minicomputer in the On-Line Training Center and operate on small samples (3000 to 5000 references) of over 60 databases supplied by the database vendors. The emulation software is continually updated to reflect changes in the systems being emulated.

Database Practice Files

An alternative to computer-assisted instruction is to use the actual search sytsem but search on a limited database, thus significantly reducing the searching costs.

The DIALOG system makes available a set of low cost training files called ONTAP (Online Training and Practice). They contain a command set that computes and displays a recall and precision score online for each final answer set retrieved by the searcher for predefined questions. New searchers can practice on the system alone or in groups as part of a training session, and performance can be evaluated immediately. The ONTAP databases are offered at a minimum searching cost and allow almost all searching capabilities except offline printing (12).

The Information Bank has established a similar training database called *Tutorial*. It, too, permits all of the normal functions of searching on the full system, but operates on a limited database at significantly less cost than the full system.

Computer as Online Assistant

Another computer-assisted training approach is to use a computer as intermediary between the searching system and the searcher. Individualized Instruction for Data Access (IIDA), developed by Drexel University and the Franklin Institute, is designed to support end users in doing their own searching, although it has potential for training as well. Transmissions from the terminal to the search system and from the search system to the terminal go through an intermediate computer. IIDA will identify problems the searcher is having and provide further explanation; if the searcher requires additional help, it can be requested from IIDA (13).

USER MANUALS AND OTHER LITERATURE-BASED TRAINING

Many searchers learn to use search systems through informal training methods, especially user manuals. Search system vendors and database producers generate a large amount of documentation. While system documentation is an important source of information, most of it is designed for reference, not for training. In this section, useful documentation is reviewed.

Search Service and Database Vendor Produced Literature

Search system vendors produce brochures of databases available on the system, extensive user manuals covering search system protocol, searching aids and tips, user guides on databases offered (including information on how the databases are loaded, and tips on searching them), and vocabulary guides and thesauri for databases. Some database vendors offer similar user guides, vocabulary lists, and other types of training literature in support of their files. The basic user manuals supplied by search system vendors contain information on how to dial into the system and how to construct search strategies, and descriptions of available databases.

Although user manuals are the best source of system-specific information, training courses offered by search service vendors and database producers sometimes supply user guides and training materials that are not otherwise available. These training materials are the primary sources of information necessary for effectively searching individual databases.

Search aids should describe the coverage of the database, the journals and other sources that are indexed and/or abstracted, and editorial policies about what is included. Descriptions of the source materials are useful as well; they can provide more information about the content of materials than a simple title listing of sources can. Search aids frequently include tips on when and why to use specialized fields such as classification codes, or when to use freely selected terms rather than a controlled vocabulary.

Textbook Sources

Textbooks serve a useful training purpose by providing a basic foundation in the principles of searching, database selection, search strategy construction, and resources for continuing training. These basic principles cannot be covered in depth in short training sessions. On the other hand, textbooks cannot be as current with the protocol of individual search systems and the content of specific databases. Textbooks are most helpful if used in conjunction with current user manuals from specific systems and with hands-on experience.

Journal Literature

Several journal publications are directed at the practicing searcher of online information retrieval systems. The best known of these are ONLINE and DATABASE, published in the United States, and *Online Review*, published in England. ONLINE is produced quarterly and carries articles contributed by searchers and scholars. The articles cover a variety of topics of interest, such as searching techniques in specialized databases, equipment reviews, reference interviewing techniques, and managerial and accounting topics. DATABASE is also oriented to practical issues, but covers information related only to databases. It contains topical articles on specific databases, searching techniques, news and notes, calendars of database training, and other features. *Online Review* is similar to ONLINE in that it covers the entire range of searching needs. It is more international in scope, carrying articles about searching activities in England and Europe as well as in the United States. It also compiles an international bibliography of online searching that is updated regularly.

ONLINE and DATABASE are published by Online, Inc., which sponsors an annual conference on online searching. These are intensive, three day conferences with sessions on a wide variety of topics of interest to searchers. *Online Review* also sponsors an annual conference, the "International Online Information Meeting." That conference is more scholarly in nature, with presentations of formal papers and the publication of conference proceedings. All three publications are excellent sources of information for keeping up to date and improving searching skills.

Many other journal publications in the field of library and information science and in topical subject areas carry articles about online searching. Regular columns on online searching also appear in standard library reference services publications.

Considerations in Selecting Searching Aids

While searching aids can be obtained from a variety of sources, much duplication in content and coverage exists, particularly in the area of databases. Very few of these publications are free, and some are rather expensive. If descriptions of a database are available from both the search service vendor and the database vendor, the manager should decide if both are needed, and if not, which one should be purchased.

One of the first considerations in such a selection is how frequently the database is used; if frequent, the cost of additional tools may be justified more readily. Search aids may be more indispensible for a database requiring the use of a controlled vocabulary than for one that can be searched by free text. Even in a controlled vocabulary database, if the thesaurus is available online and the database is used infrequently, it may be possible to dispense with an expensive printed thesaurus.

In examining specific materials, consideration should be given to features that will improve the coverage already available in the search center's collection. Vocabulary control materials should include explanations of specific coding systems such as classification codes, along with numerous examples and illustrations. Discussions of editorial policy should also be included, such as codes that are listed but no longer used. The most helpful listings give the dates that specific codes or vocabulary terms have been in use.

It is important to have source lists for commonly used databases (and for infrequently used ones as well, if it can be afforded). The source list is the only way to know the coverage of the database precisely, and a good one should be more than just a list of titles. It may include some description of the source items, publisher name, address and subscription costs; starting date of coverage in the database, and whether coverage of the source item is selective or cover-to-cover.

Vocabulary aids are needed particularly for controlled vocabulary databases. They vary from simple lists of terms to complete thesauri with "see also" references, scope notes, term relationships, and frequency counts of term usage.

In all search aids, explanations should be clear and concise and should include many examples. Search hints are also helpful by providing the expertise that otherwise requires years of experimentation to learn. The desired information should be easy and quick to find. This is especially important when searching online and ready reference aids are needed.

SUMMARY

Thorough training is the key to effective use of online information retrieval systems. Searchers must be well grounded both in the basic principles of information retrieval and in the use of specific systems and databases. They should continually update and improve their skills in order to remain effective.

A wide variety of types and sources exist for both initial and advanced training and for maintaining searching skills. Several questions remain to be answered about the best methods of training and the evaluation of materials. As awareness and use of online systems increase, a larger number and variety of training resources will become available.

REFERENCES AND NOTES

1. Wanger, Judith. *Overview of Training Needs and Opportunities*. Paper presented at the American Library Association Annual Meeting, Dallas, Texas, June 24, 1979.
2. Wanger, Judith; Cuadra, Carlos A.; and Fishburn, Mary. *Impact of On-Line Retrieval Services: A Survey of Users, 1974-1975*. Santa Monica, CA: System Development Corp., 1976. NTIS: PB-268 591/5SL.
3. For further discussion, see: Kuroki, Kristyn. "Online Regional and On-Site Training Opportunities in the Lockheed, SDC and BRS Systems and Their Databases." *ONLINE*, Vol. 3, No. 3 (1979), p. 36-49.
4. Kassebaum, Laura and Leiter, Joseph. "Training and Continuing Education for On-Line Searching." *Medical Informatics*, Vol. 3, No. 3 (1978), p. 165-175.
5. Keenan, Stella. *The Design of Training Courses for the Users of and Specialists in Networked Information Services*. Loughborough, Eng.: University of Loughborough, Dept. of Library Information Science, 1977.
6. Caruso, Elaine and Griffiths, John. "A TRAINER for Online Systems." *ONLINE*, Vol. 1, No. 1 (1977), p. 26-34.
7. Eisenberg, Laura J.; Standing, Roy A.; Tidball, Charles S.; and Leiter, Joseph. "*MEDLEARN*: A Computer-Assisted Instruction Program for MEDLARS." *Bulletin of the Medical Library Association*, Vol. 66, No. 1 (1978), p. 6-13.

8. Moghdam, Dineh. "User Training for On-Line Information Retrieval Systems." *Journal of the American Society for Information Science*, Vol. 26, No. 3 (1975), p. 184-188.
9. Caruso, Dorothy Elaine. "Tutorial Programs for Operation of On-Line Retrieval Systems." *Journal of Chemical Documentation*, Vol. 10, No. 2 (1970), p. 98-105.
10. Soben, P. and Tidball, C. S. "MEDLEARN, an Orientation to MEDLINE." *Bulletin of the Medical Library Association*, Vol. 62, No. 2 (1974), p. 92-94.
11. Duncan, Elizabeth E.; Klingensmith, Patricia J.; and Ross, Nina M. "An Exercise in Utility." *ONLINE*, Vol. 4, No. 1 (1980), p. 64-67.
12. Bourne, Charles P. and Robinson, Jo. "Education and Training for Computer-Based Reference Services: Review of Training Efforts to Date." *Journal of the American Society for Information Science*, Vol. 31, No. 1 (1980), p. 31-35.
13. Meadow, Charles T. "Computer as Search Intermediary." *ONLINE*, Vol. 3, No. 3 (1979), p. 54-59.

BIBLIOGRAPHY

Bellardo, Trudi; Kennedy, Gail; Tremoulet, Gretchen. "On-Line Bibliographic System Instruction: A Classroom Experience and Evaluation." *Journal of Education for Librarianship*, Vol. 19, No. 1 (1978), p. 21-31.

Borgman, Christine L.; Trapani, Jean-Ellen M. "Novice User Training on PIRETS (Pittsburgh Information Retrieval System)." *Proceedings of the American Society for Information Science*, 38th Annual Meeting, Vol. 12, Washington, DC: ASIS, 1975, p. 149-151.

Borko, Harold. "Teaching On-Line Retrieval Systems at the University of California, Los Angeles." *Information Processing and Management*, Vol. 14, No. 6 (1978), p. 477-480.

Bourne, Charles P.; Robinson, Jo. "Education and Training for Computer-Based Reference Services: Review of Training Efforts to Date." *Journal of the American Society for Information Science*, Vol. 31, No. 1 (1980), p. 25-35.

Caruso, Dorothy Elaine. "Tutorial Programs for Operation of On-Line Retrieval Systems." *Journal of Chemical Documentation*, Vol. 10, No. 2 (1970), p. 98-105.

Caruso, Elaine; Griffiths, John. "A TRAINER for Online Systems." *ONLINE*, Vol. 1, No. 1 (1977), p. 26-34.

Duncan, Elizabeth E.; Klingensmith, Patricia J.; Ross, Nina. "An Exercise in Utility." *ONLINE*, Vol. 4, No. 1 (1980), p. 64-67.

Eisenberg, Laura J.; Standing, Roy A.; Tidball, Charles S.; Leiter, Joseph. "*MEDLEARN*: A Computer-Assisted Instruction Program for MEDLARS." *Bulletin of the Medical Library Association*, Vol. 66, No. 1 (1978), p. 6-13.

Harter, Stephen P. "An Assessment of the Instruction Provided by Library Schools in Online Searching." *Information Processing and Management*, Vol. 15 (1979), p. 71-75.

Kassebaum, Laura; Leiter, Joseph. "Training and Continuing Education for On-Line Searching." *Medical Informatics*, Vol. 3, No. 3 (1978), p. 165-175.

Keenan, Stella. "Promote, Educate or Train?" *Proceedings of the 3rd International Online Information Meeting*. New York: Learned Information, 1979, p. 343-349.

Knapp, Sara D.; Gavryck, Jacquelyn A. "Computer Based Reference Service – A Course Taught by Practitioners." *ONLINE*, Vol. 2, No. 2 (1978), p. 65-76.

McCarn, Davis B. "Online Systems – Techniques and Services." In Williams, Martha E., ed., *Annual Review of Information Science and Technology*, Vol. 13. White Plains, NY: Knowledge Industry Publications, 1978.

Meadow, Charles T. "Computer as Search Intermediary." *ONLINE*, Vol. 3, No. 3 (1979), p. 54-59.

Mignon, Edmond. "Position Paper No. 1: Proposed Standards for Education in Online Searching in the Professional Librarianship Curriculum." In Mignon, Edmond, ed., *New Techniques in the Teaching of Online Searching: An Institute for Library Educators*, June, 1978. ED 157553.

Mignon, Edmond. "Position Paper No. 2: On the Relationship between Library Schools, Search Service Vendors, and Database Producers." In Mignon, Edmond, ed., *New Techniques in the Teaching of Online Searching: An Institute for Library Educators*, June, 1978. ED 006493.

Moghdam, Dineh. "User Training for On-Line Information Retrieval Systems." *Journal of the American Society for Information Science*, Vol. 26, No. 3 (1975), p. 184-188.

Moghdam, Dineh. *The New York Times Information Bank in an Academic Environment and a Computer-Assisted Tutorial for Its Non-Specialist Users.* Doctoral dissertation, University of Pittsburgh, Graduate School of Library and Information Science, 1974.

Slavens, Thomas P.; Ruby, Marc E. "Teaching Library Science Students to do Bibliographic Searches of Automated Databases." *RQ*, Vol. 13, No. 1 (1978), p. 39-41.

Soben, P.; Tidball, C. S. "MEDLEARN, An Orientation to MEDLINE." *Bulletin of the Medical Library Association*, Vol. 62, No. 2 (1974), p. 92-94.

Unruh, Betty. "Database User Aids and Materials – A Study." *Proceedings of the 3rd International Online Information Meeting.* New York: Learned Information, 1979, p. 351-372.

Vickery, Alina; Batten, A. M. "Development of Multi-Media Teaching Packages for User Education in Online Retrieval Systems." *Online Review*, Vol. 2, No. 4 (1978), p. 367-374.

Wanger, Judith. "Education and Training for Online Systems." In Williams, Martha E., ed., *Annual Review of Information Science and Technology*, Vol. 14. White Plains, NY: Knowledge Industry Publications, 1979.

Wanger, Judith; Cuadra, Carlos A.; Fishburn, Mary. *Impact of On-Line Retrieval Services: A Survey of Users, 1974-1975.* Santa Monica, CA: System Development Corp., 1976. NTIS: PB-268 591/5SL.

Index

For Product Safety Concerns and Information please contact our EU representative GPSR@taylorandfrancis.com
Taylor & Francis Verlag GmbH, Kaufingerstraße 24, 80331 München, Germany

www.ingramcontent.com/pod-product-compliance
Ingram Content Group UK Ltd.
Pitfield, Milton Keynes, MK11 3LW, UK
UKHW021303190926
475701UK00009B/642

* 9 7 8 0 3 6 7 4 5 1 8 1 3 *